FURNITURE STUDIO 4

Focus on Materials

ANNUAL JOURNAL OF THE FURNITURE SOCIETY

Also in the Furniture Studio series:

Furniture Studio 1: The Heart of the Functional Arts (1999)
Furniture Studio 2: Tradition in Contemporary Furniture (2001)
Furniture Studio 3: Furniture Makers Exploring Digital Technologies (2005)

THE FURNITURE SOCIETY

The Furniture Society is a non-profit organization
whose mission is to advance the art of furniture making
by inspiring creativity, promoting excellence, and fostering
understanding of this art and its place in society.

Furniture Studio 4
Focus on Materials
ISBN 096710043-7
Copyright ©2006 by The Furniture Society
All rights reserved

Editor: John Kelsey
Design and layout: Maura J. Zimmer
Copy editor: Kate Garrenson

Printed in Canada

First printing: September 2006

Library of Congress Cataloging-in-Publication Data

Furniture studio 4 : focus on materials / edited by John Kelsey.
    p. cm. -- (Furniture studio ; 4)
  Includes bibliographical references and index.
  ISBN 0-9671004-3-7 (alk. paper)
1. Furniture--Materials. I. Kelsey, John, 1946- II. Title: Focus on materials.
  NK2231.F63 2006
  684.1--dc22

                        2006019366

THE FURNITURE SOCIETY
111 Grovewood Road
Asheville, NC 28801
Phone: 828-255-1949; fax 828-255-1950
www.furnituresociety.org

Rights inquiries:
Kelsey Editorial Services
PO Box 909
Bethel, CT 06801
info@johnkelsey.com

Book trade orders:
Independent Publishers Group (IPG)
814 North Franklin St.
Chicago, IL 60610
312-337-0747 fax 312-337-5985
www.ipgbook.com

Preface

Welcome to the fourth volume in The Furniture Society's journal series. This volume builds on the success of *Furniture Studio 3: Furniture Makers Exploring Digital Technologies* and continues the Society's support for critical writing in the field of studio furniture. It has been a pleasure to see this series grow in both content and profile within the field. Our editorial board, which consists of a group of volunteers from within the Society's membership along with Editor John Kelsey, creates on an annual basis one of the more remarkable publications in the craft field.

This will be the second year that this journal has been a benefit of membership in The Furniture Society. We are fortunate to have this publication and its distribution supported by a grant given anonymously. Without this incredible support, we would be unable to publish and to offer this publication as a benefit of membership.

Feedback is an important aspect of any publication and I would like to invite you to let me know what you think about this publication. Please send your comments to me at director@furnituresociety.org.

—*Andrew H. Glasgow, Executive Director, The Furniture Society*

Foreword

Gail Fredell's story on page 56, about hitting a wall in her own development as a furniture artist, points out the necessity of trusting yourself and your own creative instincts. Practiced craft skills are essential, as is education, responsible criticism, and marketplace support. But in the end, creative development as a designer/maker can only result from a conversation between you and whatever you decide to make.

Not so with a journal such as *Furniture Studio,* which belongs to all members of The Furniture Society. We're governed by an Editorial Advisory Board (facing page), and we've attempted to illuminate our process and thinking by way of the Editor's Notes you'll find along with many of the essays in this volume. This is not a closed conversation. Do you like what's been published here? Do you have ideas of your own to advance? Would you enjoy participating more directly?

Please accept the invitation extended to you by Andrew Glasgow and by me: please do join the conversation about Furniture Studio and tell us what you think. Please send publicity material about your work, images of your work, and story ideas you might like to develop, to Furniture Studio, PO Box 909, Bethel CT 06801, or to me online at johnkelsey@aol.com.

—*John Kelsey, Editor, Furniture Studio*

Mission

Furniture Studio, the annual journal of The Furniture Society, presents images and ideas about studio furniture, furniture making and design, and furniture makers/artists. By placing studio furniture in an artistic, social, cultural, and historical context, the journal promotes a better understanding of the work and inspires continuing advancement in the art of furniture making.

Policy

It is the editorial policy of *Furniture Studio* to represent all aspects of the studio furniture field, reflecting its diversity as to age, gender, materials, and stylistic preference. A broad range of connoisseurs, writers, critics, and historians from within and outside the field offers reflection and opinion in the journal. The journal encourages the work of emerging designers, makers, and writers.

Mission and policy statement adopted by The Furniture Society Editorial Advisory Board, May 2004

```
R.I.P.
Arthur Espenet Carpenter
1920-2006
```

Art Carpenter received The Furniture Society's lifetime achievement award in 2001 (page 124).

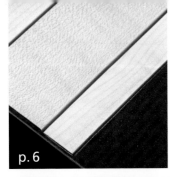

p. 6

p. 16

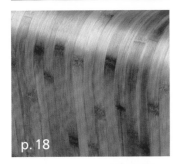

p. 18

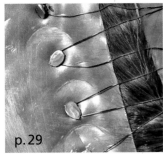

p. 29

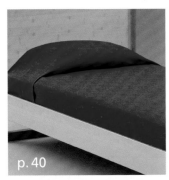

p. 40

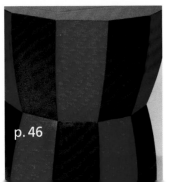

p. 46

Contents

p. 56

p. 66

p. 79

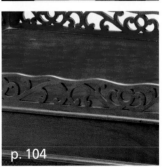

p. 92

p. 104

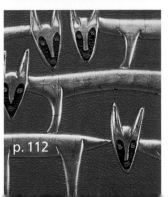

p. 112

Material Dexterity

Furniture makers fluent in metal, concrete and stone as well as wood

by Jonathan Binzen

Wood is such a compelling material for the furniture maker that it's easy to spend a career building with nothing else. Wood's range of textures, colors, and aromas, its strength and warmth, its adaptability—these attributes, along with the panoply of specialized machines, tools, and techniques required to manipulate wood with mastery—tie the maker to the material in a monogamous marriage.

But over the last decade I've noticed a rising number of furniture makers who demonstrate a native speaker's fluency in more than one material. Mixing other materials with wood in furniture is nothing new, of course, as anyone from King Tut to Garry Knox Bennett could tell you. There is all sorts of experimentation with materials taking place at present—furniture is being made with everything from sorghum stalks to recycled rain boots—and it can be fizzy fun to see outré materials put to use. But what's more deeply impressive is to see furniture makers going beyond serial experimentation and committing themselves to other materials with the disciplined passion and technical virtuosity most often reserved for wood.

This story features designers who combine wood with metal, concrete, glass, and stone. I sought work that showed not so much the promise of new or unusual materials but rather the power of a few materials handled with dexterity and discernment. In the best work of this sort I find an exquisite tension—as in the best musical ensembles— between the discrete character of each component and the unified effect of the whole composition.

detail of *Carbon*
by Peter Harrison, p. 11

Isaac Arms
Sheet steel with wooden slats

Wood and steel came together for Isaac Arms at the University of Wisconsin, Madison, where he got his MFA. His first training had been in woodworking, but sculpture classes exposed him to metal and then a workshop at Anderson Ranch with Jim and Melanie Cole gave him the skills and the impetus to design furniture out of steel. His first pieces were all steel, but he soon realized that for the user, "steel is often harsh, cold, and hard. I wanted to bring the warmth and tactile quality of wood" to pieces made predominantly of metal. The result was a group of benches made of sheet steel with slatted wooden seats that combine sculptural power with inviting functionality.

Arms, now living in Bozeman, Montana, designs on the computer using a CAD-like program. All the angles for the steel parts are automatically calculated and he sends a computer file to a metal shop with a CNC laser cutter. In return he gets a stack of perfectly cut parts in ⅛-inch sheet steel, which he welds together. The welding, grinding, and sanding, he says, "is not too enjoyable. It's a messy process, and really loud. But it goes quick. A day and a half or two days and it's done."

To bring an element of the unpredictable to the symmetrical designs, Arms cuts the seat slats in random widths. Despite their bulk, the benches are relatively light, weighing about 120 pounds apiece. That's a lot of presence per pound.

right, with detail above:
Slump with Slats (2005)
Isaac Arms
Steel, cherry; 64 inches
x 17 inches x 17 inches.
Photo: Bill Lemke

top: *Parquet Table* (1993)
Peter Fleming
Afrormosia, sand-cast aluminum, green slate;
82 inches x 34 inches x 18 inches.
Photo: Jeremy Jones

bottom: *Tortoise Coffee Table* (1996)
Peter Fleming
French walnut, patinated sand-cast bronze;
52 inches x 52 inches x 15 inches.
Photo: Peter Fleming

Peter Fleming
Mechanical connections replace glued joints

For the first ten years after setting up his furniture shop Peter Fleming worked almost exclusively in wood. But in the early '90s he began to bring metal, stone, and glass into his pieces. Now he can't imagine working only wood. "It isn't so much that I'm rejecting a purist approach," he says. "There's just something great about looking at the wide range of options available and selecting materials based on their inherent qualities."

Working with a blend of materials, Fleming points out, requires "a different vernacular of construction. You are always thinking about how things can come apart and be put back together." Since adhesives often are not successful,

mechanical connections typically replace glued joints. That creates an engineering challenge, but it satisfies the need for different materials to be finished separately and assembled afterward, and it also simplifies any future repairs.

Fleming often pairs metal legs with wooden casework. For legs like those on his *Tortoise Coffee Table,* which are hollow, thin-walled, and open on the inside face, he makes a fiberglass model and has it sand-cast. He typically leaves the pebbly texture of the castings untouched on curved surfaces, machining it smooth on flat faces required for joints or where he wants a visual contrast.

Fleming is head of the wood department at Sheridan College of Crafts and Design near Toronto.

Tall Sideboard (1994)
Rob Hare
Maple, cherry, forged steel;
84 inches x 90 inches x 22 inches.
Photo: Ralph Gabriner

Rob Hare
Components that fit like puzzle pieces

For Rob Hare, making things with wood and metal was practically bred in the bone. The Waldorf school in New Hampshire where he spent his high school years in the '60s had its own sawmill, and students helped fell trees, cut them into lumber, and turn the boards into buildings for the school. The curriculum was limber enough to let him advance his mechanical and metalworking skills (and snag his first set of wheels) by rebuilding an antique car on campus. When he showed a strong interest in art, his teachers turned him loose, and his dorm room became an atelier where he produced sculpture out of soldered copper and carved ebony. After a decade as a sculptor working mostly in metal, in the '80s Hare began building cabinets and furniture. He worked at first in wood but soon began to add metal elements.

Virtually all Hare's work now incorporates both materials. In a typical case piece, an interlocking forged-steel skeleton supports wooden casework. The wood and metal components fit together like a puzzle, the whole unit becoming rigid only when the last piece is fitted into place. Hare rarely uses fasteners between the wood and metal parts, favoring instead a system of notches and mortises that he likens to the slotted cards kids play with. The pieces can be knocked down by reversing the process without so much as unscrewing a bolt.

Hare forges much of his own hardware, but resists purely decorative embellishments in any material. "If it doesn't function," he says, "I'm not interested in it." Looking back over his career, Hare says, "the wood and metal were never far apart. I might wander off in one direction or the other for a while, but they always come back together."

Peter Harrison
A vastly expanded vocabulary

Glue was slowing Peter Harrison down. Several years out of Rochester Institute of Technology, where he was trained in traditional woodworking skills, Harrison stood back to consider the economic viability of producing wood furniture. It struck him that glued joints presented an impediment to efficiency, since they were laborious to create, time-consuming to fit, clamp, dry, and clean up, and potentially problematic in terms of alignment, sanding, and finishing.

So, for largely practical reasons, Harrison set out to design some pieces that didn't have glued joints. But the new pieces, he says, "morphed into a look and a language that I like more than the work I was making before." Harrison's vocabulary expanded to include cast concrete, stainless steel, sheet aluminum, aircraft cable, and various off-the-shelf and custom fasteners. In addition

to speeding up the building process, Harrison says, "the interaction of different materials can make each element visually stronger."

Harrison keeps it basic with each material—using wood, concrete, and metal in elemental geometric shapes and in their natural colors. The joints in most of his pieces consist of bolts and threaded inserts. Asked whether the curved stainless steel rods and aircraft cables serve a structural purpose, Harrison says, "Not much of one, but in my work the visual function is as important as the actual function. I try not to have any element there just because it's functional. Every element should be a harmonious part of the piece whether it's serving to support it or just to visually fulfill it."

facing page, top: Argon (2006)
Peter Harrison
Mahogany, stainless steel cable, aluminum, concrete, glass;
36 inches x 36 inches x 16 inches.
Photo: Robert Storm

facing page, bottom: Carbon (2006)
Peter Harrison
Mahogany, stainless steel cable, aluminum, concrete, pencil;
48 inches x 36 inches x 10 inches.
Photo: Robert Storm

below: Jupiter (2004)
Peter Harrison
Mahogany, stainless steel, aluminum, concrete;
50.5 inches x 16 inches x 10.5 inches.
Photo: Shay Stephens

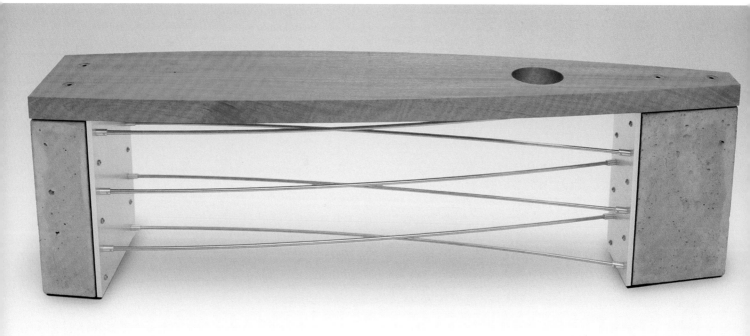

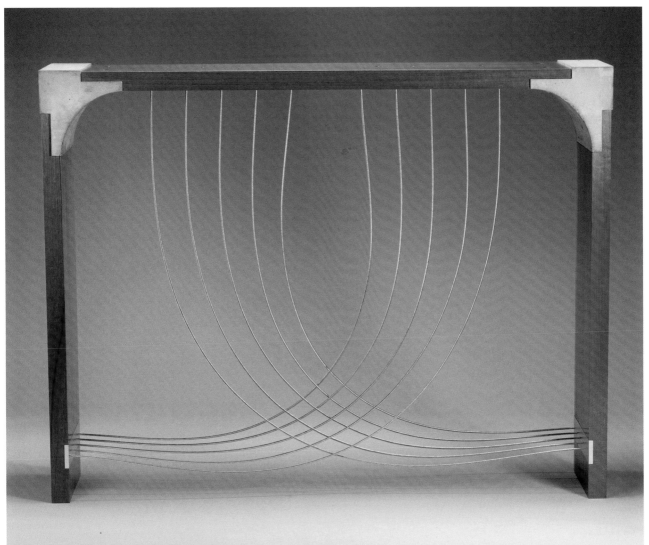

above: Greek Bench (2003)
Chris Martin
Cherry, steel, leather, milk paint;
46 inches x 24 inches x 20 inches.
Photo: George Ensley

left: In Balance Table (2003)
Chris Martin
Reclaimed redwood, steel, concrete,
twisted wire, brass;
21 inches x 29 inches x 22 inches.
Photo: George Ensley

Chris Martin
Paring down to essences

Chris Martin is professor of wood design at Iowa State University, but his taste in materials takes him far beyond the one mentioned in his title. He works with forged and welded steel, has taught himself to anodize aluminum, and has experimented with cast resins and carbon fiber. He has made jewelry out of Corian and furniture out of rubber. His current work in furniture typically combines wood with metal, and sometimes with concrete.

Martin loves the effects obtainable with steel, but concedes that they come at some cost. "When you weld," he says, "the metal expands and contracts and bends in unpredictable ways. You have to give in to what the material is going to do, but try to keep it under control enough that it ends up looking something like what you designed." At the same time, he finds steel forgiving in that if you make a mistake you can simply cut out or fill the error and re-weld.

With an interest in so many materials, the temptation for Martin is to keep adding and making increasingly complex pieces. In past work he took that direction, but, he says, "with the current work I'm aiming to pare it down to its essence."

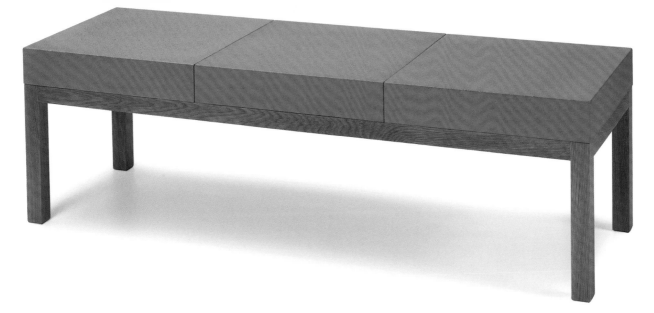

Filbert Coffee Table (2004)
Peter Sandback
Polymerized concrete, white oak;
54 inches x 18 inches x 17 inches.
Photo: Ed Thomas

Peter Sandback
Lightweight concrete

When the wave of concrete countertops broke across California a few years ago, Peter Sandback caught it. With an MFA in sculpture from the Art Institute of Chicago, he was making art while supporting himself by building stretchers for painters' canvases. His girlfriend (now his wife) was working in a small furniture store in Berkeley, and he began making tables with concrete tops and selling them there. They sold well, so he found a much larger outlet in San Francisco.

The economics were good—the process was simple and the material was much less expensive than wood—but the tables were heavy, weighing up to 300 pounds. When Sandback and his wife decided to move east, he realized he would lose his West Coast clients unless he could lighten the tables dramatically. After a year of experimenting, he perfected his current process, in which he casts a half-inch layer of polymerized cement over a block of rigid foam. Even with some tops as thick as 8 or 10 inches, his tables now weigh between 30 and 120 pounds.

Sandback's second challenge was to find a surface finish that would address concrete's problems with porosity and staining. His hard-won solution is an enticingly smooth surface and a modified urethane finish. He also pigments the concrete in some four dozen colors. Now settled in Rindge, New Hampshire, Sandback has a woodworker friend build the table bases, but he does all the concrete work and assembling himself. And then he ships his tables all over the country.

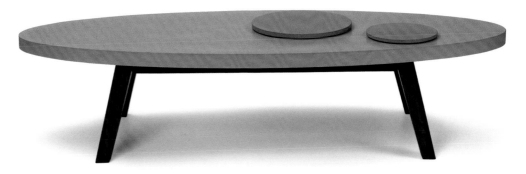

Arlington Coffee Table (2004)
Peter Sandback
Polymerized concrete, walnut; 62 inches x 23 inches x 13.5 inches.
Photo: Ed Thomas

Jaffe Table (2005)
Bailey Heck
Cherry, stainless steel, glass;
138 inches x 36 inches
x 30 inches.
Photo: Bevan Walker

Bailey Heck
Elemental wood married to steel

For Bailey Heck, furniture design is interwoven with architecture. He learned to make furniture while studying architecture at the University of Virginia, and right from the start he was blending wood, metal and glass in compositions that, he says, "brought the articulation of building structures down to a smaller scale."

In architecture school most design is hypothetical, and Heck was drawn to furniture for what he calls "the almost instant gratification. You could design something and see it materialize in a matter of weeks." Now that he is a practicing architect in

Manhattan, Heck remains committed to furniture and has a shop in the Brooklyn Navy Yard.

Heck's pieces are notable for their marriage of elemental forms in wood with crisp and complex brackets, struts, and braces made from surgical stainless steel. On a conceptual level, Heck intends his furniture to evoke the interaction between man and nature. Wood, in his scheme, expresses the natural world, and Heck endows it with monolithic, curvilinear forms that might have been eroded rather than built. In contrast, he uses steel in shiny, sharp-edged, linear shapes that speak of manufacture.

Douglas Thayer
Simplicity can be complicated

Douglas Thayer builds garden benches almost exclusively, and the basic program could hardly be more rudimentary: two legs of cast concrete, a plank seat. Thayer was building full-bore furniture in his father's basement workshop before he was out of junior high school. Motors, metalwork, and all things mechanical were also on his daily agenda. Then, at Rochester Institute of Technology, Thayer ratcheted up his already considerable skills with wood and metal. Yet a dozen years after graduating, he makes furniture that would seem to require only a sliver of his expertise.

But as designers inevitably discover, simplicity can be complicated. In Thayer's benches the weight of the legs and the purity of the shapes require strong mechanical connections and structural reinforcements that must be buried in the concrete or in the underside of the seat. Each leg can weigh 80 pounds or more, so the benches must knock down for shipping and be easy to assemble. The minimal format also carries aesthetic demands. It can accept subtle modifications and embellishments, but resists dramatic measures: step too far over the line and the natural presence of the piece is spoiled.

Thayer finds working in his strictly defined format bracingly diverse. "One day I'm welding rebar," he says, "threading studs and cutting steel. The next day I might be working on a beautifully figured

top: Wilma (1998)
Douglas Thayer
Mahogany, cast concrete, copper;
50 inches x 13 inches x 16 inches.
Photo: Douglas Thayer

above: Dan (2000)
Douglas Thayer
Reclaimed redwood, cast concrete, copper inlay;
32 inches x 11 inches x 16 inches.
Photo: Eric Salisbury

mahogany top. Then it's on to making a good mold. And the next day I might have the cement mixer going. I'm still fresh and excited about the work because of the diversity." And the narrow scope of work seems to be a spur to creativity—his notebook teems with ideas for new benches.

Stacks and Stacks of Unusual Stuff

by Jonathan Binzen

For a designer, surely one of the most pulse-quickening rooms in the country is a small, subscription-based library tucked away on the second floor of a building on the lower west side of Manhattan. That is where you'll find Material Connexion, a nine-year-old company dedicated to discovering and cataloguing innovative materials from all realms of manufacture and all parts of the world.

Material Connexion has a small display gallery and a ring of offices for its 20 employees, but for most visitors the heart of the matter is the library. There, samples and descriptions of some 1,200 materials are mounted on display boards and arranged on stack-like shelves. Each display board carries a cogent description of the material's composition, properties, and uses, and also lists contact information for the manufacturer or supplier.

The library serves a diverse group of members. On a typical day a furniture maker might share the stacks with a sculptor, a toy maker, and a car designer. Cross-pollination is at the core of the Material Connexion's mission. Dr. Andrew Dent, an engaging English materials scientist who is the library's director, says that some of the best results come when a designer finds a new application for a material that has already been put to use in another field. He showed me an Air Jordan sneaker that incorporated a flexible woven synthetic material originally developed to sheath bundled cables. Nike designers found the stuff at Material Connexion and made it the centerpiece of a new design (of which they sold some 5 million pairs).

On a recent visit, I examined scores of materials I'd never seen before that seemed to offer fascinating possibilities for furniture making. There were sheet goods made from everything from straw to salvaged aluminum. One laminate was composed of bark from dead trees, another consisted of an ⅛-inch layer of stone (limestone, marble, granite) glued to a ¼-inch layer of fiberglass-reinforced epoxy or

The main stacks at Material Connexion contain samples and descriptions of 1,200 innovative materials from around the world.

glass. Yet another, made in either MDF or plywood, contained a center layer of rubber or leather. When a v-shaped cut is made in the board, the center layer acts like a hinge, so light-duty boxes and cases can be made without further joining. The library catalogues innovative processes as well as materials. One process can convert a digital file into a surface pattern on either gypsum-based polymer tile or ceramic tile.

In addition to the materials in the main library, there are 1,800 more mounted in the same format and stored in an adjacent area, and they can be accessed with the help of a librarian. All 3,000 materials are included in Material Connexion's

 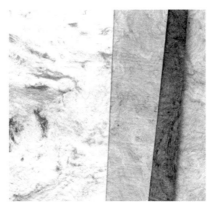 

One of a raft of unusual sheet goods in the library, BioFiber Wheat is made from crop residue and has good water resistance and screw-holding ability. It also represents the library's strong emphasis on green materials.

A thin and flexible sheet material, Barkskin is made by hand-pounding bark cut from dead trees. Sheets of the naturally colored bark are available up to 4 feet x 8 feet.

This product, 3-F Board, has a layer of leather in the center. When a v-shaped groove is routed across the sheet, the leather serves as a hinge. Developed as a low-cost means of making displays and point-of-purchase stands, it is now finding uses in furniture.

searchable digital database, which is accessible through terminals in the library and via the Internet.

The collection grows by 40 or 50 materials per month. Material Connexion staff are constantly trawling for prospective additions, and many other materials come in over the transom from manufacturers and others, who do not pay for inclusion but must be juried into the collection. Each month, Dr. Dent sifts the best candidates and selects 80 to 100 to present at a meeting of the library's jury. The jurors, who are invited to serve and who volunteer their expertise, include architects, engineers, material scientists, artists, industrial designers, and fashion designers. By the end of the evening, 40 or 50 new materials are accepted for the collection. And soon afterward a PDF file containing photos and descriptions of the newly inducted materials is winging its way via email to each of Material Connexion's members. Materials are only removed from the collection if they are no longer available.

Material Connexion membership is on a yearly basis and the cost varies with the number of users and the level of access. An individual with access both to the physical library and its online counterpart pays $450 per year (active members of The Furniture Society receive a 15% discount).

A company buying full access for four users might pay $1,500 per year, and a corporation buying access for an unlimited number of users pays as much as $15,000. Rates are lower for strictly online access to the collection. For an individual, a year of online access is $200 (the discount does not apply to this rate). For students, the Material Connexion offers an online-only rate of $100; for teachers, the same membership is $150. The library also has group arrangements with many colleges.

I found the online database easy and enjoyable to use, and it would seem well worth the cost of membership. But there is no substitute for seeing and feeling the samples in person—I felt like I was getting behind-the-scenes tours of the R&D departments of hundreds of cutting-edge companies in the course of an hour. For those who live too far away to make junkets to New York feasible, the librarians will do some research for you. And you might be in luck on another score— Material Connexion has opened branches in Cologne, Milan, and Bangkok, and more are on the way.

Material Connexion
127 West 25th Street, 2nd Floor
New York, NY 10001
(212) 842-2050
www.materialconnexion.com

The Legacy of the Golden Spruce

A personal journey to sustainability through a smaller business

by John Wiggers

My own deep affinity for forests and trees began long before the rainforest crises of the 1980s. This is because on three occasions as a boy/young man a tree played a significant role in saving my life: once from lightning, once from drowning, and once from an automobile wreck. This story tells how a tree changed the course of my life.

In 1990 I was a furniture maker with a small shop near Toronto, Canada. Simply doing my work and being an active father to three young children seemed more than I could handle. But life had other plans. One day I came home to find my oldest

son, then almost 4, in tears. He had been watching a cartoon on television about environmental superheroes that defeated an evil furniture maker who was gobbling up the rainforest with a giant machine. My son wanted to know if my work was also destroying the rainforest. As I tried to explain, I realized that I wasn't sure whether my materials had been harvested in any sort of responsible manner. Even as a small-scale woodworker I knew I was having some kind of impact on the forest— however tiny that impact was.

Communication by design—John Wiggers created this Biedermeier-inspired design, called Rainforest Desk, in 1990 as an awareness-raising piece to encourage the responsible use of tropical and temperate hardwoods. Photo: Tony vander Cruysen

My questions led me to Andrew Poynter of A&M Wood Specialty, a founder of the Woodworkers' Alliance for Rainforest Protection (WARP). He gave me a number of answers, which then inspired me to create an awareness-raising piece called the *Rainforest Desk*. This desk was later auctioned off at the International Interior Design Exposition in Toronto, to help raise funds for WARP.

By 1992 the economic downturn had a devastating effect on my business, then a five-man shop. I came very close to losing everything—including my home. Today I recall this experience as a profound inner awakening. In the ensuing years, as my business gradually recovered, such issues as rainforest degradation were no longer at the forefront, I was too busy with my family and my work. That changed in 1997 with an incident on Haida Gwaii that became an international news story, because it involved an act of eco-terrorism against a sacred tree known as the Golden Spruce.

facing page: **Prophetic tree**—The magnificent radiance of the Golden Spruce defied all conventional scientific explanation. In Haida folklore this sacred tree embodied the spirit of a young boy, along with a prophecy that if the tree was allowed to die, the Earth as we know it would soon follow. Photo: Russ Heinl

The Golden Spruce

Haida Gwaii (also known as the Queen Charlotte Islands) lies 100 miles off the northwest coast of British Columbia. Covered in lush temperate rainforest, these islands provide habitat for a broad range of unique plant, animal, fish, and bird species. For at least 10,000 years, Haida Gwaii has also been home to the Haida First Nation, a powerful and enduring tribe famous for their warrior culture, myths, and totemic art forms.

One enduring mystical story derived from Haida folklore is that of K'iid K'iyaas, which loosely translates as "Old Tree." The legend tells of a boy who was disrespectful of nature's ways. When his village was destroyed by a snowstorm, only the boy and his grandfather were able to flee. Despite warnings not to look back, the boy disobeyed and instantly his arms were turned into branches and his legs became roots, and he was transformed

Editor's note—*As you will see, this is an intensely personal story told with some passion by John Wiggers, who makes furniture in Toronto. Wiggers also chose the artists to present in the accompanying photos. To see more of Wiggers's work and learn more about his company, please go online to www.wiggersfurniture.com.*

What we do not understand, we fear. And what we fear, we destroy.
—Black Elk, Oglala Sioux

into a magnificent golden spruce tree that became sacred to the Haida people.

Although genetically a Sitka spruce, this tree's survival defied all conventional scientific explanation. Lacking carotenoid, a sort of arboreal sunscreen, the Golden Spruce should have withered and died. Instead, it flourished for more than 300 years on the bank of the Yakoun River—until January 1997 when an unemployed forester named Thomas Grant Hadwin cut the tree down and sent a Unabomber-type manifesto to the Haida First Nation, environmentalists, and several newspapers.

A vocal critic of logging practices, Hadwin was particularly angered by the hypocrisy of clear-cutting hundreds of thousands of trees, while professing to be good corporate citizens by cordoning off a small segment of rainforest around the Golden Spruce. Hadwin's letter declared, "I didn't enjoy butchering this magnificent old plant, but you apparently needed a wake-up call that even a university-trained professional should be able to understand." Hadwin was arrested and charged, but he mysteriously disappeared before ever coming to trial.

The Haida were devastated because they considered themselves responsible for the tree's stewardship. Even more upsetting, the felling of the Golden Spruce heralded the fulfilment of an ancient prophecy that said if the tree is allowed to die, the Earth as we know it is soon to follow. When I first read this story, I felt rocked to the very core of my being and I vowed that if I ever got out to the West Coast I would pay my respects to this tree.

Shortly afterward I learned that an organization called Smartwood was looking to certify woodworkers in accordance with the guidelines of the FSC. Without hesitation I signed up and on Earth Day 1998 I became one of the first furniture makers in the world to be certified to FSC chain-of-custody guidelines. To mark the occasion I designed and built the *Andiroba Armoire,*

another awareness-raising piece, using some of the first wood to have been certified as sustainably harvested. In 1999 the World Wildlife Fund invited me to display this piece at their "Forest Economy 2000" symposium in Mainz, Germany.

In 2000 I was elected to the board of FSC Canada, and with an upcoming board meeting in Vancouver, I now had my opportunity to visit the Golden Spruce. I made my way northward, and finally found myself standing at the very spot I had promised myself three years earlier—and I could only laugh, for the Golden Spruce lay on the west bank of the Yakoun River, while I was standing on the east bank, separated by a wide expanse of deep, frigid water.

"Ridiculous," I thought. "After feeling so driven to come here, and at a time when I am so busy at work and cannot afford to take the time away—here I am in some remote corner of a rainforest and not even close to the tree I had come to see. Why?"

I looked back up the trail at a massive tree that had recently fallen in a windstorm. Perhaps the purpose of coming out to see the Golden Spruce might actually be to bring me to this other tree. These two trees, about the same height and age, had spent the last several hundred years growing up together, albeit on opposite banks of the river. As I made my way back to the wind-felled tree, a profound feeling of connectedness began to overwhelm me. Looking at the pool of water where the tree once stood, it seemed as if Earth herself had been opened up.

I remember vividly the absolute silence of the undisturbed, ancient forest. The only sounds I could hear were the occasional call of a raven, and the distant rolling thunder of heavy logging trucks. In the stillness I looked down to see, reflected onto the water at the base of the fallen tree, four very distinct images. These images were not figments of my imagination or strange reflections of light, because they were very concise and were visible from many angles. The images formed a crude circle. One figure was of a salmon, one was of a baby bird pleading to be fed, the third was of a man's face with owl-like features, and the fourth appeared to be an ancient skull. I got the sense that this symbolized Mother Earth.

As I made my way back to the logging road, I thought, "This is crazy. I am going to have a hard enough time trying to explain why I went here at all—let alone describe what I just saw." For the longest time I told no one about what had happened.

Business Was Booming

Business was booming and it was easy to keep myself distracted. My shop now employed 20 people working overtime, and I was preparing to build a new 25,000 sq. ft. shop, which would have allowed the business to grow to more than double. My customers were begging for more capacity, and the bank was giving me the green light, but something didn't feel right. All of this extra business was not the result of any genius on my part, I was simply being asked to make furniture at a level that far exceeded my capacity. Remembering the lean times, I was reluctant to turn anything down, so I took on more than I could handle. I was overwhelmed with quotes and production schedules, cash flow projections and trouble-shooting—without myself doing any of the actual work that was the rationale for being in business in the first place. Having taken on a life of its own, the business was racing out of control.

Shortly after my return from Haida Gwaii I walked around the lot where I was planning to build. It was a cold, clear and sunny day and as I trudged through the powdery snow I heard the repeated shrieks of a hawk coming from a nearby line of trees. As I approached the sounds a flurry of feathers greeted me, and I leaped back just in time to avoid a face-full of talons.

A red-tailed hawk had been feasting on a rabbit on the other side of the snow bank. In its panic to flee, the hawk and I had a near head-on collision. What added to the surreal feeling were the impressions of the hawk's wings as it flapped up the snow bank.

Trees and man—The freeform shape of the *Andiroba Armoire* resembles a sculptural hybrid between human and tree-like forms. Each of the individually sculpted drawers has discretely integrated finger pulls.
Photo: John Glos

The imprints looked like ascending angels. This incident felt ominous, so I called a native friend who explained that a red-tailed hawk is considered a messenger. But a messenger of what, I wondered. The only thing I knew for certain was that I had to step back to avoid a collision. But what was it I had to step back from?

I quickly realized that this was all connected to my plans to build. Fortunately I had an escape clause in my deal to purchase the land, so I bailed, and within a month found a smaller industrial space that I could renovate instead. As I soon discovered,

Painted vision—Wiggers commissioned Donna Bisschop to paint the images he had seen on the trail to the Golden Spruce. When the painting arrived on Haida Gwaii in 2002, one elder remarked that "it looks like the spirit is being pulled from the fish." Several weeks later, Haida spokesman Leo Gagnon reported that the salmon had failed to return to the Yakoun River for the annual spawn. Photo: John Glos

experience to Donna she not only insisted on being the one to make the painting, but she also refused to accept payment—saying it was necessary that no money change hands. I now felt selfish at the thought of keeping the painting for myself, so we jointly decided to donate the artwork to the FSC who, in turn, would give the painting to the Haida as a gesture of hope over the loss of their sacred tree.

A presentation was scheduled for April 2002 at the Forest Leadership Forum in Atlanta, an international forestry congress being hosted by the World Wildlife Fund. An elder named Leo Gagnon was brought out to receive the painting on behalf of the Haida, and I spoke publicly about my experiences.

the timing couldn't have been better. Business softened early in 2001, and I scaled back to what is now a seven-man shop. One unanticipated benefit is that I have since been able to focus more on doing the work I love—designing and building my own furniture.

Had it not been for the near collision with the red-tailed hawk I would probably have proceeded with the new building, creating an overhead so high that I would have gone out of business. In walking my own path, I have discovered that my pursuit of sustainability on a global level has also manifested quite unexpectedly as a direct and sustainable transformation of my own life and vocation. The paths have woven together.

The Haida Speak

By December 2001, a year after my trip to Haida Gwaii, the memory of that experience continued to gnaw at me. If I left things for too long my memory would fade, so I decided to commission the artist Donna Bisschop to paint the memory to canvas for me to hang in my office. After describing my

When Leo spoke, it was clear that the gesture had moved him deeply. He spoke of K'iid K'iyaas and the deep sense of loss that the Haida and many other indigenous peoples have felt over the demise of this sacred tree. He then went on to describe how a magazine writer had recently visited the islands to write a story about what happened to the tree (the story, entitled "The Golden Bough," was published in *The New Yorker* magazine in November, 2002).

As the writer was leaving Haida Gwaii, Leo told him to call if he ever had a dream about an eagle. And as Leo was walking out the door to travel to Atlanta, the writer telephoned. He said that the previous night he had a dream about an eagle, and not only that, but his wife had the very same dream. In the dream an eagle soars down from the sky. Landing on the beach the eagle transforms into a man, who then walks out onto the surface of the water. Peering below the surface he sees the body of a man. Leo interpreted this to mean that the spirit of the Golden Spruce is happy that its story is being told.

After the presentation I asked Leo about the prophecy surrounding the sacred tree. He said that according to Haida legend the tree has now fallen for a third time, and this would herald a great change for the Earth. I pointed out to him that a team of biologists had taken grafts from its living root and nursed a seedling that has now been transplanted at the base of the fallen tree. So, technically, the tree is still alive by way of the seedling.

"It doesn't matter," Leo somberly replied. "Perhaps it makes people feel better to think they have saved the tree, but the reality is that it has now fallen and the great change is now under way."

above: **Underwater wood**—*Anomaly Side Table* by William Stranger of Pasadena, California has a top made of birch that was reclaimed from the bottom of Lake Superior. This dense first-growth wood is much finer in texture than hardwoods generally available today. The legs are made of birch that came from a well-managed forest certified by the Forest Stewardship Council (FSC). The finish is non-toxic linseed oil.
Photo: William Stranger

below: **Reclaimed wood**—Brian Fireman of Asheville, North Carolina used reclaimed pine flooring to create the top of his majestic *Elk Table.* The sculpted cherry base is made of wood salvaged from a storm-felled tree. The finish is a hand rubbed oil and wax blend.
Photo: Steve Mann

Locally harvested wood—*Treble Zero Chair* by Petter Bjorn Southall of Bridport, Dorset, England, is one example of Southall's emphasis on using sustainably grown timbers native to the UK. Southall also takes care to avoid the use of glue and artificial finishes, which he feels is his response to a polluted, mass-produced, and careless world. Photo: Petter B. Southall

Restorative forestry—
Mark Leach of Riner, Virginia sculpted his *Filly and Foal* tables out of walnut stumps and black locust wood that was horse-logged using a traditional model of restorative forestry developed by the Menominee Indian tribe. The horses are able to skid out the logs with minimal disturbance of the forest soil, and over time these methods actually improve the health of the forest through selectively harvesting weaker trees—thereby providing space for younger, healthier trees. Photo: Mark Leach

Sustainable forestry—In Central America Scott Landis, one of the founders of the Woodworker's Alliance for Rainforest Protection, has helped spearhead a community-based sustainable forestry initiative called Greenwood/Madera Verde. Its mission is to increase the value of the forest to its local inhabitants through appropriate woodworking technology. In turn, the forest dwellers below are able to earn more by managing their forest sustainably than they would make from conventional agriculture or destructive logging.
Photo: Scott Landis

Sustainable bamboo—Anthony Marschak of Oakland, California uses bamboo to craft furniture such as this elegant *Spring Chair.* Bamboo is considered a sustainable alternative to wood because it is actually a grass and one of the fastest growing plants on earth— growing up to four feet per day in some cases.
Photo: Robert Kong

Recycled wood—*Clutch* by Peter Loh of Bellevue, WA is made from salvaged and recycled Douglas fir with a glass top. Loh says the inspiration for the table came from clutches of ladybug eggs laid on the underside of leaves.

Materials: What Is Sustainably Harvested Timber?

There is a lot of confusion about what is sustainably harvested timber, and about how the issues of forestry practices in a warming world affect the small-time furniture maker. Here is a short history of the movement for sustainable forestry.

In 1987 The World Commission on Environment and Development issued a landmark report entitled Our Common Future which included a definition of sustainable development:

"Development that meets the needs of the present without compromising the ability of future generations to meet their own needs."

This concept reflects the growing global awareness of destructive logging practices such as clear-cutting in endangered rainforests, an issue already familiar to studio furniture makers who used tropical hardwoods. In 1989, as a response, a grass-roots non-profit organization of woodworkers and related industry professionals was formed to address wood-harvesting issues in general and tropical rainforest issues in particular. This group became known as the Woodworkers' Alliance for Rainforest Protection (WARP).

An early awareness-raising effort initiated by WARP was an exhibit and catalog of furniture built using sustainable materials and processes. Known as Conservation by Design (ISBN #0-9638593-0-7) the book/catalog was edited by WARP founder Scott Landis, and the touring exhibition opened at the Rhode Island School of Design in 1993. It featured thought-provoking works by such talents as Silas Kopf, Kristina Madsen, Timothy Philbrick, and the late John Shipstad.

All connected—Furniture maker Michael Brolly contributed this piece, entitled *Our Mother Hangs in the Balance* (1992), to the Conservation by Design exhibit organized by the Woodworkers' Alliance for Rainforest Protection in 1993. The bat's brass tongue holds it in the flower. Remove the bat, and the tree, which supports the plant, falls down— a symbol of the interconnectedness of all things and actions. Photo: David Haas

The first WARP conference in 1990 determined that for sustainability to succeed in the marketplace there would need to be standards. This led to the creation in 1993 of the Forest Stewardship Council (FSC), an international not-for-profit organization whose founders included WARP plus environmental groups such as Greenpeace, The Sierra Club, and World Wildlife Fund. Its mandate is to protect the world's forests through globally recognized principles of responsible forest stewardship. (WARP, meanwhile, grew to become the Good Wood Alliance, which later transformed yet again to become the Certified Forest Products Council (CFPC) and then Metafore, a group that encourages sustainable forestry practices via market forces.)

The FSC and others have done much work on the sensitive issue of defining what is a sustainable forest. In addition to yield, sustainability should include a broad spectrum of environmental and social concerns, both for life now and in the future. Clear-cutting the forest and replanting the trees is not enough by itself. The broader impact of forestry practices on wildlife and overall biodiversity, herbicide and pesticide use, water quality, direct and indirect employment related to the forest, and the rights of indigenous people who live in the forest, must all be considered.

What makes the FSC unique among forest certification systems is its use of independent third-party audits and its embrace of the rights of indigenous peoples to utilize the forests for their culture, livelihood, and spirituality. By 2005 the FSC had national initiatives in 34 countries, with a total of forest area of 51,320,494 hectares under protection. Of equal importance, the very existence of FSC has spawned the creation of several competing forest certification systems such as the Sustainable Forestry Initiative (SFI), Canadian Standards Association (CSA), and the pan-European organization Programme for the Endorsement of Forest Certification (PEFC). It seems that mere presence of the FSC as the most comprehensive of all the certification systems has pushed the other systems to raise their own bars of excellence to become "more like FSC."

The FSC label is the only certified wood accepted under the U.S. Green Building Council's stringent LEED (Leadership in Energy and Environmental Design) standard. In 2004 FSC was also awarded the first ever Alcan Prize for Sustainability for its success in promoting sustainable development on a global scale. The tiny initiative that began as

WARP in 1989 has become a force for transforming the global forest landscape for the better. When furniture makers tell me they are only small players and don't really make a difference, my response is, "Take a look at what WARP has managed to accomplish."

In spite of these noble efforts to promote sustainability in the world, great volumes of illegally cut timber currently make their way to low-cost off-shore manufacturing operations. These companies process this stolen wood by the container-load for export to Europe and North America. By 1999 these unsustainable practices had become so severe in the hardwood garden furniture industry that a not-for-profit organization called Tropical Forest Trust (TFT) was created specifically to combat this trade. TFT has transformed an entire segment of the furniture industry to sustainable practices by promoting the use of FSC certified woods. So far, other market segments have been slower to follow suit, and many consumers unwittingly support unsustainable practices by basing their furniture-buying decisions on sticker price, not true cost.

Meanwhile, as emerging economies such as China continue to industrialize, new challenges emerge. China, in 1999, transitioned from being a net food exporter to a net food importer, creating massive new demand for globalized commodities such as soy beans. In 2005 the greatest single factor affecting the growing rate of deforestation in Brazil was the razing of rainforest for soybean farms. To make matters worse, the burning of these forests produces massive quantities of greenhouse gases. By some estimates burning forests now make up 20% of all manmade CO_2 gases that contribute to global warming. To say that things are unbalanced is an understatement.

—*John Wiggers*

What Can Anyone Do?

To furniture makers who wish to support sustainable forestry practices, I would like to make the following seven suggestions.

First, use less wood and choose it carefully. Use veneer instead of solid wood and look for certified woods from well-managed forests or plantations. Avoid seriously depleted or endangered species, and avoid wood from old growth forests. Contact an arborist to find locally sourced woods from salvaged trees when possible.

Second, experiment with lesser-known species. Hundreds of beautiful tropical timbers have barely been tested. Their use can bring more value to the forest and to the people who manage it responsibly.

Third, use recycled wood. Look for buildings slated for demolition as well as for packing crates and pallets, many of which are made of tropical hardwoods.

Fourth, plant a tree. An increase in resources anywhere reduces pressure on resources everywhere. However, don't plant just any tree. Help enhance the natural bio-diversity of your area by planting indigenous trees. Try planting tree species that are under pressure and at risk of extinction (or may have already gone extinct) in your area.

Fifth, join the Forest Stewardship Council (FSC), and choose FSC-certified sustainably harvested materials whenever you possibly can. The FSC provides reliable information about responsible timber management and wood use.

Sixth, make an effort to research and better understand the belief systems of the indigenous peoples. Many indigenous tribes have developed systems of beliefs that allow them to live within the bounds of natural law and create sustainable societies that have lasted thousands of years. We can learn much from their example.

Seventh, and perhaps most important, communicate to others by means of your designs. Design is powerful. We see design as beauty in the sleek lines of a classic automobile; we hear it in the lilt of soothing music; we feel it in texture, we smell it in fragrance; and in the case of a culinary masterpiece, we experience great design as a feast that simultaneously ignites our senses. Architectural and interior design is primarily visual and tactile, yet its power to inspire is by no means inconsequential. Maya Lin's Vietnam Memorial in Washington, for example, is a geometrically simple design that arouses deep feelings of sorrow, awe, and humility.

This ability to influence and inspire others through design can be seized as an opportunity to effect positive change. Studio furniture makers can build a legacy of sustainability into every piece they make. If nothing else this simply makes good business sense. In an increasingly competitive marketplace, it is ever more necessary for studio furniture makers to communicate the personal touch and the love for what they do that makes their creations unique and special.

In my own work I emphasize the use of veneers, lesser known wood species, FSC certified woods, and low-volatile finishes. In some of my recent pieces, such as *Ellipse II Table* below, I have also begun to incorporate unusual woods that have been traditionally used for holistic healing in ancient and indigenous cultures. My intent is to help people see forests as more than standing inventories of vertical timber storage. By understanding trees and forests better, we may better understand our interconnectedness with all living things.

—John Wiggers

Unusual woods—*Ellipse II Table* (2006), by John Wiggers, is made of a little known species of wood called Chaquiro. This wood is FSC-certified and its use helps to sustain an indigenous community living along the Amazon River in Brazil. The finish is a blend of natural oils and tree sap extracts. Photo: Lorne Chapman

The View from Beyond the Edge

Tasmanian makers compare notes with Americans

by John and Penny Smith, captions by Oscar Fitzgerald

Tasmania sits geographically on the very edge of the world. The underbelly of Down Under, it has been referred to as "a forgotten teardrop at the bottom of Australia," and it has occasionally been left off the national map. However, this relative isolation has also protected it from uncontrolled development, and preserved much of its seductive charm.

With its reputation for the clean-and-green production of fine foods and wines, Tasmania provides a tourist haven for Australians and overseas visitors who seek a calm respite from the big city blues, and a refuelling of the spirit. Its tranquil environment and gentle lifestyle is beguiling, and one could be forgiven for thinking that little stirs in this forgotten Eden.

But Tasmania, more so than any other state in Australia, has a dark and troubled history, in some ways signified by the harsh beauty and inherent dangers of its many remaining wild places. Its treatment and near-total genocide of its indigenous people casts a long and dark shadow. This past is still felt today, and contrasts starkly with the sheer magnificence of the landscape.

Even based in the state capital of Hobart, one is constantly reminded of the close proximity to the bush. The mountains, rivers and forests that spill across the land from the rugged wild west coast to the more sublime east coast form a majestic backdrop for looking out at the rest of the world.

This sense of being on the edge applies equally to Tasmania's east coast as to the west coast of America, which looks toward it across the Pacific. This highlights the similarities and parallels between the United States and Australia—in their histories, landscapes, and attitudes.

This mirage contains shared ghosts of European colonialism—of population growth through immigration, and a frontiersman pioneer attitude of looking forward to a self-made future, leaving history behind. Both cultures have similar legacies of social discord when it comes to finding meaningful reconciliation with the indigenous cultures. And as edge-dwellers, the majority of our population clinging to the coastlines, we

Editor's note—"Convergence: Crossing the Divide" is an exhibition of studio furniture by eight artists from Tasmania and eight from North America, most of whom had visited Tasmania to teach. The United States tour of "Convergence" began at the Oceanside Museum of Art, San Diego, during the Furniture Society's 2005 conference. It then traveled to the San Francisco Museum of Craft + Design before being presented at SOFA Chicago by the Furniture Society.

This article is adapted from catalogue remarks by the Tasmanian co-curators, John and Penny Smith, with a selection of formal furniture-in-space photographs from the exhibition catalogue. The extended captions accompanying the photos were prepared by Oscar Fitzgerald, Renwick scholar at the Smithsonian Institution and a member of the Furniture Studio editorial advisory board.

Just when you think that culture worldwide has been flattened by global media and the Internet, something like this exhibition comes along to shatter such a comfortable notion. The Tasmanian furniture shown here, despite the strong influence left behind by visiting artist/teachers from America and Britain, reflects a different history and viewpoint. Tasmania truly is over the edge, and so is some of its studio furniture.

—John Kelsey

have slowly been sucked into our adopted lands—emotionally and metaphorically.

These elements are expressed in studio furniture, not only in a regional sense but also in a dialogue with "the other" beyond our shores. Tasmanian furniture has retained some of the traditional skills inherited from our colonial past. Tasmanian studio furniture is also overlaid with the expressive freedom and sculptural narrative that has become so well-developed in North America. In Tasmania the growth of creativity is inevitably influenced by the natural environment, which remains a spiritual touchstone to the artists working here.

The island relationship of Tasmania's "edge" to the "beyond" remains intriguing. Much of Tasmanian design is inspired by the notion of the island's regional particularity, in dialogue with international design generality. The local is thus informed by the global. This vision of standing on the edge—looking inward and outward simultaneously—is shared by many Tasmanian furniture artists.

The key educational program from which the majority of furniture artists have emerged in Tasmania over the past three decades has deliberately drawn input from Britain initially and the United States latterly. Summer schools had been conducted in Tasmania during the late 1970s by the furniture maker Don McKinley from Sheridan College in Canada. The furniture program at the University of Tasmania was established in 1981 through residencies by two British artists, Ashley Cartwright and Hugh Scriven. This program was based upon the designer-maker practice that was emerging in Britain at the time. Later, furniture artists from the United States—many of them represented in this exhibition—were sought to inject an alternative viewpoint.

As you might expect, and as you can see in this exhibition, these American artists not only left their mark on Tasmanian studio furniture, they also took something of it away with them. Jon Brooks and Kristina Madsen, in particular, found their personal aesthetic and artistic motivations significantly changed by their sojourns Down Under.

The Tasmanian work, though diverse, can be seen to have some things in common. It all, to varying degrees, incorporates a sense of narrative. The most direct would be Patrick Hall's theatrical cabinets, each like a little stage set, relating personal stories accompanied by poetic text engraved into their surfaces that draw upon nostalgia and emotional memory. The narrative is equally clear in the work of Wayne Hudson, Kevin Perkins, and Peter Prasil, as is their concern for spotlighting the edge—whether of plant and animal extinction, craft and technology, materials usage, or personal risk-taking.

The view from the edge, if you look hard enough, far enough, and for long enough, is the distorted reflection of yourself looking back at you. Looking back, to wherever home is from another edge on the other side, helps to clarify this distorted reflection—bringing into focus the reality that we are not a disjointed and multifaceted series of others, but simply one-another, converging into a unified spirit.

The View from Tasmania

Goose with Hutch (2004)
Kevin Perkins
Silky oak, Huon pine, painted King Billy pine, frosted wire glass, Tasmanian oak, automotive paint; 61 in. high x 13.5 in. deep x 39 in. long.
Photo: Peter Whyte

Trained as a joiner, Kevin Perkins is best known for his interiors including St. Patrick's Cathedral in New South Wales, Australia, and the prime minister's suite in Canberra's new Parliament House. His personal work presents an archive of endangered Tasmanian species, both trees and birds. Now protected and on the rebound, the Cape Barren goose on its protective hutch is his signature piece, although over the past 15 years he has rendered other endangered birds such as the coot and the swamp hen. His early geese were more abstract, but this one, carved from a single piece of King Billy pine, is painted realistically. The carved underbelly suggests the ripples of water in its native habitat off Cape Barren Island between Tasmania and the mainland.

The painted shelves are Tasmanian oak while the biscuit-joined doors and dovetailed sides of the hutch are locally grown silky oak, both members of the eucalyptus family. The drawer fronts are Huon pine which, along with the North American bristlecone pine, is the longest-living tree in the world, some as old as 4,000 years. Highly resistant to the toredo marine borer, it was over-harvested for boat building. This stock came from old, clear-cut forest stumps that have a highly figured grain. Although the slanted shelves recall Post-modern work by Ettore Sottsass and others, Perkins conceived the design as a practical way to store bottles of grog or books without the need for bookends.

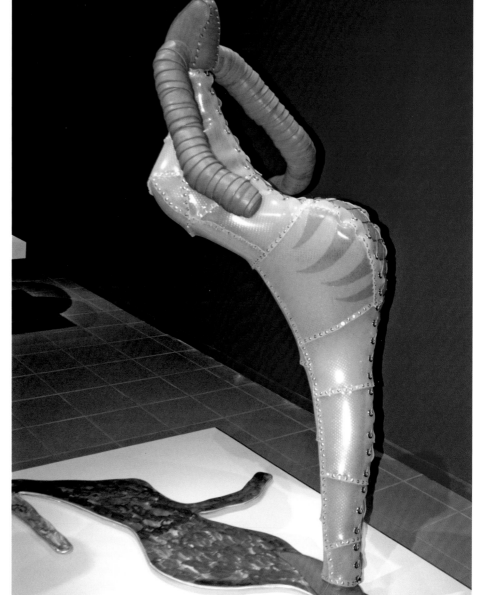

Dancing Tigress (2004)
Wayne Z. Hudson
(detail below)
Aluminum, steel, leather,
fabric, silicon rubber,
stainless steel;
65 in. high x 33.5 in. wide
x 45.5 in. deep.
Photo: Peter Whyte

The figure—which Wayne Hudson calls a "prop for social discourse"—
recalls a friend Hudson met at a disco. She was a sexy dancer with dramatic
gestures, who had once studied ballet. As is characteristic of his other sculptures,
this piece explores the relationship between male and female: how they meet,
their mating rituals, their courting gestures and their romance. In this case the
female is designed for males to lean upon for support and comfort—as they
often do in real life.

Hudson's eleven earlier, abstract metal leaning props were influenced technically
by his internship with Albert Paley in 1993 and 1997. This piece also harks back
to his earlier training as an upholsterer. The complex steel-rod armature is first
covered with chicken wire, then canvas, then different densities of foam, then
Dacron wool, and finally a red fabric meant for a cocktail dress. The fabric is
visible under the silicon rubber covering which he cut out like a dress pattern,
riveted together and cinched up like a corset with stainless steel wire. The tiger
stripes on the hips are textured black vinyl, and all the other exposed surfaces
are covered with orange leather. The wrapping of the arms echoes the metal-
wrapping technique Hudson learned from Paley. The base was band-sawn from
a sheet of aluminum, following the outline of the shadow cast by the body.

Rock (2005)
Peter Walker
Cherry;
30 in. high x 32 in. wide x 22 in. deep.
Photo: Erik Gould

Raised in Sydney and trained at the School of Art at the University of Tasmania (with Jon Brooks), Peter Walker now teaches at the Rhode Island School of Design. In the fall of 2003 he had the opportunity to explore new work at the Haystack Mountain School of Crafts in Deer Isle, Maine. He was struck by the similarities of the rugged landscape in Maine to his native Tasmania, both in appearance and in how people respond to it. Camping on the beach and inspired by its rocks, Walker decided to use a huge boulder as a form to wrap with thin strips of cherry. He clamped and glued the strips to each other until they retained their shape without the supporting rock, though mostly preserving its outline. He carried the piece home and worked on it intermittently for the next year until one day he knew it was done. The ends of each strip are hidden so that the shape appears to be formed by one continuous length of wood.

Walker's work has been a mixture of large sculptures often using salvaged timber beams in combination with steel and concrete, and furniture commissions for both individual and commercial use. Recently, he has moved into smaller work and has begun making another piece using the same technique of gluing up strips of wood over a form. His method recalls traditional basket-making, and the shape brings to mind the ubiquitous lobster traps found along the Maine coast, but it was the natural environment itself that inspire *Rock*.

Duo (2005)
Ross Straker
Laminated plywood, closed-cell foam, stainless steel, kiln-polished glass;
28 in. high x 27 in. wide x 75 in. long.
Photo: Peter Whyte

Duo takes its name from the dual nature of the piece, a chaise on the front end and a chair on the other end, something like a loveseat. The seating material is cell foam, a smooth-textured material with a natural ripple effect, used for packing. He stacked 50 sheets together on a plywood base and fastened them with elastic cord terminating in plastic buttons covered with flame-polished glass discs. If one layer of cell foam is damaged it can easily be stripped off to expose a fresh sheet. Unable to bend the plywood frame as a single sheet, Straker cut it into four sections, vacuum-formed them and then biscuit-joined them. The eight layers of eighth-inch bent plywood rest on tapered, U-shaped, polished stainless steel strips, a signature element that creates a bright focal point while also protecting the plywood edge. The other edges are sanded smooth but are not edge banded. Straker's work explores the theme of opposites: geometric and linear, solid and void, black and white, soft and hard, expensive and cheap. Clean, modern design, he observes, is more challenging than traditional work where ornament can be used to cover up mistakes.

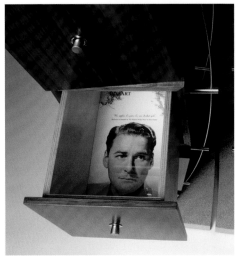

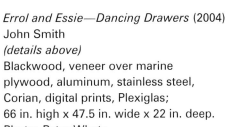

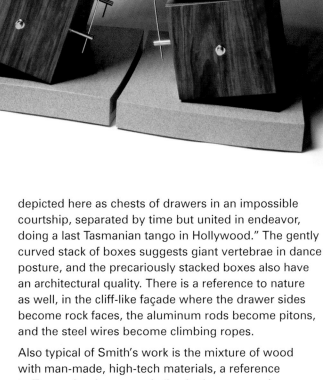

Errol and Essie—Dancing Drawers (2004)
John Smith
(details above)
Blackwood, veneer over marine
plywood, aluminum, stainless steel,
Corian, digital prints, Plexiglas;
66 in. high x 47.5 in. wide x 22 in. deep.
Photo: Peter Whyte

John Smith trained as a furniture designer in England and immigrated to Hobart in 1970 to establish a three-dimensional design course at the Tasmanian School of Art, now part of the University of Tasmania. That program has blossomed into the furniture design studio that Smith now heads, and his graduates form the core of Australia's internationally known studio furniture fraternity.

Each of the five drawers in the taller case contains a digital image of Errol Flynn and the drawers in the shorter one have Essie's likeness looking up at Errol while they dance. Errol Flynn was a Tasmanian native who went to Hollywood, and Essie Davis, a rising young star whom Smith knew as a young girl, is following in those footsteps. The dancing drawers are homage to "these celebrated creative exports from Tasmania,

depicted here as chests of drawers in an impossible courtship, separated by time but united in endeavor, doing a last Tasmanian tango in Hollywood." The gently curved stack of boxes suggests giant vertebrae in dance posture, and the precariously stacked boxes also have an architectural quality. There is a reference to nature as well, in the cliff-like façade where the drawer sides become rock faces, the aluminum rods become pitons, and the steel wires become climbing ropes.

Also typical of Smith's work is the mixture of wood with man-made, high-tech materials, a reference to Tasmania where people live in the man-made environment of Hobart but enjoy the surrounding bush. The biscuit-joined, plywood cases and drawer fronts are veneered with blackwood, cut from locally grown sustainable forests.

Lure (2005)
Patrick Hall
(detail above)
Plywood, aluminum, glass,
collected fishing reels,
LED lighting; 71.5 in. high
x 43 in. wide x 21 in. deep.
Photo: Peter Whyte

Sepia faces scattered on the kitchen table,
Descendants each anchored by lines of blue brio.
A knotted rope of marriages, births, deaths,
Blood and name descends into black giving her
measurement and depth.

This sampling from Patrick Hall's poetry, diamond-etched into the glass drawer fronts of his cabinet, gives a sense of the complexity and multiple meaning conveyed by his furniture. The spirit levels, inset into a band at the top of the cabinet, reinforce the idea of descending into the mysterious depths beneath the water level. Twelve antique fishing reels screwed to the side are ingeniously connected to each of the 12 drawers so that cranking a reel opens a drawer. It is a modern version of a Renaissance cabinet of curiosity. As the fisherman

hopefully casts his line into the unknown, so the viewer opens each drawer with the same sense of anticipation. The lures, attached to each drawer face and made of stainless steel mesh and lit by LEDs, are portraits of people. Like the fisherman, we choose our lure and drop our lines and sometimes we connect with other people, and sometimes we don't.

This cabinet is part of a series featuring found objects such as toy trains, cars, 78 RPM records, and family photo albums. Hall turns this mundane detritus into profound studies of human emotions. Since graduating from the Tasmanian School of Art, he and his partner, jewelry designer Di Allison, have maintained a studio in Mount Nelson, Tasmania.

Debacle 98 (2004)
Peter Prasil
Plywood, polyurethane foam, fiberglass,
automotive paint, aluminum, stainless steel;
47 in. high x 29.5 in. wide x 37.5 in. deep.
Photograph by Peter Whyte

The debacle that Peter Prasil memorializes was the
disaster that hit the Sydney-to-Hobart sailboat race
in December 1998. A fierce storm battered the yachts,
sinking six boats, drowning five sailors and causing
another 50 to be airlifted off. The fiberglass-covered,
polyurethane case recalls the sleek hull of the boats,
but also suggests a shark lurking in the water. The glass
sheet with holes bored in it represents the waterline,
an effect heightened by bubble-like shadows on the
fiberglass. The wheel on the side suggests a crank to
raise sails, but here it opens and closes a drawer in the
front of the case. The keel-like extension at the back of
the case is topped with a pencil sharpener and handle.
The plywood drawer contains about 50 sharpened
pencils, one for each of the sailors rescued from the sea.

Although he holds bachelor of fine arts and PhD degrees
from the University of Tasmania, Prasil first trained as
a tool-and-die maker in Denmark before emigrating
in the late 1970s. He machined all the aluminum and
stainless steel parts including the shapely housing for
the pencil sharpener. Prasil's work also includes benches
and tables all made of metal and fiberglass.

Beach Patterns (2005)
Mark Bishop
Slash pine plywood, Huon pine, blackwood,
stained Tasmanian oak, stainless steel, aluminium;
57 in. high x 19 in. wide x 22 in. deep.
Photo: Peter Whyte

A native of Stanley in the far northwestern part of
Tasmania, Mark Bishop left home to attend the Canberra
School of Art and learn wood turning in the 1980s, with
a stint at the Wood Turning Center in Philadelphia as part
of the international turning exchange in 1997. He returned
to Stanley 12 years ago to set up his own woodworking
shop on the beach that provides much of the inspiration
for his recent work. Although some of his pieces still
incorporate turned elements, he has for the past eight
years concentrated on cabinetmaking. The surfaces of this
series of cabinets, "domestically useable sculpture" he
calls them, are inspired by the ocean and the sand in front
of his house, in this example suggesting the ripple effect
caused by the waves lapping on the beach. Other cabinets
in the series recall a whirlpool and raindrops on a window.

Bishop routed the pattern into construction-grade slash
pine plywood, harvested from sustainable forests.
He then cut the plywood into drawer faces, and charred
and sandblasted the surface. What appears to be
prominent wood grain is really the effect of routing
into the layered plywood.

The View from North America

Picton River Chairs (2004)
Jon Brooks
Maple, stain, lacquer, colored pencil;
84 in. high x 24 in. wide x 24 in. deep.
Photo: Dean Powell

A native of New Hampshire, Jon Brooks works in a studio he built for himself outside of New Boston. He gathered the hard, curly maple for these chairs on his 185 acres of conservation land surrounding his house. After a residency at the University of Tasmania in the early 1980s, his work took a new direction. He named these chairs for the Picton River in Tasmania, a normally bucolic stream that unexpectedly turned into a torrent after a huge release of water from an upriver dam on the very day he decided to run it. The blue, water-based wash on the slats, seat, and arms suggests the river itself, while the stiles, front posts, and stretchers recall the frightening turbulence. These elements are decorated with multicolored pencil squiggles protected by six coats of lacquer. He was inspired by similar brush strokes he observed on Australian aborigine art. On another level these chairs, built as a pair and leaning lovingly toward each other, express an almost anthropomorphic affinity. It is the same attraction that Jon feels for Australia.

right, and on page 29: Miss Dovetails (2005)
Kristina Madsen
Pau amarello, maple, milk paint, gesso;
29 in. high x 41 in. wide x 13 in. deep.
Photo: David Stansbury

Kristina Madsen is best known for her delicate, lace-like carving, a style she developed after studying in Fiji with master carver Makiti Koto. While serving as an artist in residence at the University of Tasmania she began to experiment with colored surfaces. Although most of her work is stained black to highlight her carving in the Fijian manner, this chest uses color. She first painted the maple box to match the color of the green silk that lines the chest, then carved the pattern into the surface. Then she outlined the ribbons with thin, carved lines and carved the background more or less freehand. Using a tooth-brush, she filled the carved cuts with white gesso, rubbing off the excess from the painted surface. Madsen explains: "As with all of my recent work, I am using light reflected off shallow, carved facets to create the illusion of depth and dimension, in an effort to intrigue and tickle the eye." The case corners are splined miters, and the base is mortised-and-tenoned. Despite the title there is not a single dovetail in the piece—Miss Dovetails was Madsen's nickname at the University of Tasmania.

Ladderbackkcabreddal (2005)
Tom Loeser
Maple, cherry, paint; 87 in. high x 14 in. wide x 41 in. deep.
Photo: Bill Lemke

Though it is tempting to think of *Ladderbackkcabreddal* as a metaphor for the northern and southern hemispheres, Tom Loeser spent only five days in Hobart in 2000 and he says there is no connection. He was simply experimenting with double chairs. At first he designed them back-to-back, and then he hit on the idea of two chairs joined like these. They actually do sit and rock comfortably, either way up. Loeser likes the dramatic effect of black and white milk-based paint, and the slats and seats on this piece alternate between the two colors with a unifying neutral gray accent used on all the painted surfaces. The darker cherry for the seats and the rockers contrasts with the lighter maple selected for the rest of the chair. The seats are screwed to parallel stretchers, raised up slightly on shims to create the illusion that they are floating. Mortise and tenon joinery, mostly at right angles, is used throughout, with the legs and back posts formed by bent lamination. The completed piece was given three or four coats of a hand-rubbed, oil-and-varnish finish.

Growing up on a farm in northwestern Alberta, Canada, Paul Epp was always fascinated with old metal-and-wood farm tools. Seeing similar implements while a guest lecturer at the University of Tasmania in 1995 reinforced the childhood memories and became the genesis for these stools. They are first in a series that he is tentatively titling *Scenes from Childhood.* While they recall the ax handle chairs of Wharton Esherick from the 1930s and the current work of Brad Smith in Pennsylvania who uses actual farm tools such as pitchforks, Epp's work is more abstract and refined.

Untitled (2004)
Paul Epp
(left to right) Blue mahoo, Honduras rosewood, curly hard maple all with cast aluminum hardware; *(left to right)* 26 in. high x 26 in. wide x 26 in. deep; 36 in. high x 20 in. wide x 20 in. deep; 23 in. high x 16 in. wide x 16 in. deep.
Photo: Peter Paterson

Although these stools have not been put into production, Epp designed them with that possibility in mind. Like all farm tools, the tables deliberately celebrate the construction details. The cast aluminum brackets holding the legs are shaped like hollow gears. The legs are wedged between flanges and are attached snugly to the brackets with special, deep-threaded screws. Simple W-shaped brackets, which echo the shape of the undercarriage, join the top to the base.

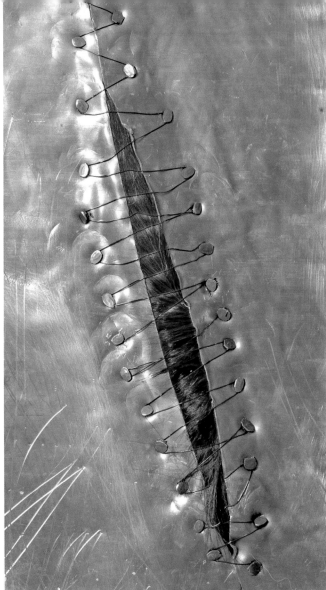

You Don't Know What You've Got 'Til It's Gone (2005)
(detail at right)
Wendy Maruyama
Polychromed mahogany, digital media, lead, fur;
50 in. high x 18 in. wide x 14 in. deep.
Photo: Michael James

Both Wendy Maruyama's cabinet and the multimedia presentation it contains are homage to the now extinct Tasmanian tiger. She explains, "Ever since I was a kid, I have always been fascinated by animals. I have always been obsessed and saddened by the extinction of animal species, especially those decimated by man." The loss of the Tasmanian tiger was brought home to her in 2000 while on a lecture tour of Australia. She learned that after the tigers were hunted to near extinction, authorities tried to save the last remaining few in zoos but with little success. Ben, the last surviving Tasmanian tiger, died of exposure when his keeper forgot to bring him in from the cold one night. None have been seen since.

Maruyama made the piece especially for the "Convergence" show. She likens the cabinet to a "Butsudan," a family shrine that is used in the Buddhist faith. The case of mahogany, whose grain telegraphs through the black paint, could easily be a lead-lined tomb or coffin. The torn and patched surface suggests that the trapped animal (whose fur is seen through the split) has fought furiously to escape only to be nailed back in. Maruyama combined still photographs and original film footage to produce a video showing Tasmanian tigers when they were still alive, along with scenes of cloud formations and the rising and setting of the moon as metaphors for the passage of time. The montage runs continuously on the small LCD screen.

Not a Lot of Bunk, but Just Enough

Furniture photos: Brian Urkevik, courtesy Adden Furniture

RISD professors tackle dorm furniture, emerge with a model for teaching

by Liisa Silander

Rosanne Somerson remembers how it all started—with a phone call from Brian Janes, director of Residence Life at Rhode Island School of Design. He wanted help with selecting furniture for a new, 500-bed student housing facility under construction on nine floors of a former bank building in downtown Providence. And despite a shoestring budget, he was looking for durable, highly functional furnishings with the character and personality to do justice to the hip interior design of the new housing. A tall order? Somerson, head

of RISD's Furniture Design Department, thought so: "I knew right away that there was nothing out there in his price range that would rise to the occasion," she said.

So Somerson did what every good designer aspires to do: she offered a better solution. If Residence Life was willing to take the risk, she and her full-time faculty colleagues in furniture design—John Dunnigan and Peter Walker—would design new furniture for the apartments, suites, and lofts in the

40   FURNITURE STUDIO

building. They knew it would be a stretch, especially since the budget couldn't budge and they had just over a year to design a complete line of industrial-strength furniture, plus find a manufacturer willing and able to produce it by the time the dorm opened.

John Dunnigan

"Although we all love our studio work, we had been intrigued with designing things for a different market," Somerson explained. "We also felt strongly that this project could show RISD how to make use of its own pool of design talent to address campus needs. And we knew it would be a good model for our students—to help them understand that the same design principles we use in making our studio work can be applied when designing for a commercial client."

Rosanne Somerson

Peter Walker

Since RISD's Furniture Design Department averages 65 undergraduate and 15 graduate students, they might have been recruited to solve the problem themselves. However, given the tight timetable and professional demands, none of the faculty involved felt it was a good fit for this project. "Our students are just that—students, not professionals," Dunnigan explained. "While the three of us deal with those kinds of issues all the time and many of our students do end up designing for industry, the schedule alone was enough to keep this from being a viable course offering."

In the end, the faculty team turned the project around in 15 months, from initial design to the

facing page: At art and design schools students frequently work on large drawings, so the dorm room desk has an unusually wide drawer. It also offers a raised gallery for tools, equipment, and other desktop clutter that too often eats up space for working and studying.

delivery of the manufactured furniture, and learned a lot in the process. Built from a new type of bamboo blockboard, a non-toxic medium-density fiberboard that is colored all the way through, and sustainably harvested solid beech from Europe, the 12-piece line includes a desk, a chair (the same design for both desk and dining purposes), beds, tables, chests, and soft seating. "It's very simple furniture with a lot of detail," Somerson said. "After much debate, we agreed to call the line Sage—a simple name to suggest both the green aspects of the design and wisdom."

Researching how students live

The story of how Sage developed from concept to completion begins in May 2004 at the Salone Internazionale del Mobile in Milan, where Somerson, Dunnigan, and Walker were accompanying their students—the only ones from an American design school invited to participate in the international furniture fair that year. One evening the professors were discussing the dorm project in an Italian bar when Dunnigan paused to ask the bartender the name of the appealing music blasting in the background. The response of "disco" in a heavy Italian accent was hardly what they expected, but the lightheartedness of the "DEEZ-co" pronunciation attached itself to the company they had decided to form to distinguish this new project from their individual studio work. Hence, DEZCO furniture design LLC was born.

After returning from abroad, the trio began work by visiting dorm rooms at RISD, MIT, and several other schools to see how today's students live. They consulted a spreadsheet from Residence Life listing the furniture items needed and the quantities of each, and questioned the logic of some of the items requested—a TV stand but no bookcase, for instance, or a dining chair as well as a desk chair. They resolved that for RISD students, in particular, the furniture needed be flexible to allow for storage of art materials and projects, while allowing for personalization of the space itself. Although

Liisa Silander is editor of the Rhode Island School of Design alumni magazine RISD Views, *where an earlier version of this story first appeared.*

Residence Life Director Janes agreed about the need for flexibility, he stipulated that the furniture should not be obviously adjustable, with little or no visible hardware, since art students keep a constant eye out for project materials and are notorious for appropriating anything they can pry loose.

The designers also set some basic parameters for themselves, agreeing that in addition to the project requirements for functionality, durability,

The three-drawer chest can be stacked to form a tall chest, or, when the accompanying bed is in its high-legged mode, one or two of them can fit underneath. The drawers slide on standard metal hardware but have rubber pulls, a natural material that feels good to the touch.

and economy, their line should be green, honest, and made in America. "The influence we exert over students who are learning from us can be enormous," Walker pointed out. Today's students arrive with a heightened awareness of environmental issues, so "we wanted to make ecological responsiveness a focus of our design to help teach them the importance of long-term approaches to materials."

The green aspects of the design evolved from two directions, Somerson explained: the need for an extremely economical use of materials and the desire to model ecologically sound design decisions. Once the designers began researching options, they rejected anything with a negative impact on

the environment. That would not only go against their own principles but would send the wrong message to students. "If there's any time that you want to showcase good design principles, it's when you're producing in large quantity," Somerson said. Even though "it's not cheap to be green," as Walker put it, "it's one of the most important aspects of design and production that we as designers can contribute to our culture." In addition, "a green design would serve us well in terms of marketing," Dunnigan noted, "since students tend to be way out front on issues like this."

DEZCO also determined that their line would "be about materials used in their true state, with honest construction," Somerson said. This immediately led them away from such "standard" solutions as medium-density fiberboard (MDF), which is low in cost but environmentally offensive to manufacture and needs an edge-band to both conceal the crumbly material and seal in dangerous gasses. Given the mass exodus to manufacturers in Asia and other inexpensive labor markets, the final prerequisite the team agreed on was to search for an appropriate American manufacturer.

Based on their dorm research, and the genesis of their company name, DEZCO briefly toyed with proposing that the RISD rooms simply be furnished with "a mattress on the floor and a disco ball," Dunnigan said with a grin. Instead, the designers immersed themselves in the project during the summer of 2004, sketching, tossing around ideas, making models, tossing out ideas. By fall they had edited their work down to two lines of about a dozen pieces each, which they presented to students, Residence Life staff, and a campus design review committee.

One of these lines (not chosen for the RISD housing project) "had a very different look, relying on sheet steel," Dunnigan explained. "Initially we thought that would be a very economical direction for manufacturing, but over the summer the price of steel skyrocketed, so we had to put it aside." Nonetheless, DEZCO hopes to revisit this line in the future and may yet develop it.

Finding the manufacturer

With valuable feedback from various campus constituents, the faculty designers selected the line that would become known as Sage before moving on to the next stage of the process—finding a good manufacturer. To simplify legal issues with the college, they proposed a straightforward agreement: DEZCO owns the intellectual property rights to the designs, which are licensed to RISD to develop in partnership with a manufacturer. The agreement was designed to help persuade senior college administrators of the benefits of this type of collaboration, in part by ensuring that "RISD will share in the royalties," Somerson said, when the line and any subsequent additions to it are marketed to other institutions nationwide. As they worked to resolve the legalities, the team had been surprised to discover that unlike scientific institutions, where research faculty routinely share intellectual property royalties, RISD had no such mechanism. "So creating a mutually beneficial relationship became one of our goals as well," Dunnigan said.

After interviewing five potential manufacturers, DEZCO chose to work with Adden Furniture in Lowell, MA, an established company known for producing high-quality furnishings for the college, university, and hospitality markets. However, given the sizable gap between Adden's basic tooling and manufacturing capabilities and the exacting demands of the Sage designs, it was as if the real journey toward a cost-effective end-product had just begun.

Enter Tom Hurd, Adden's vice president for marketing, who threw himself into working to bridge the gap between the spirit of the design and the realities of the factory floor. "Let's just say no blood was drawn," he laughed. "But seriously, there was a wonderful amount of give and take, which was good for RISD and for Adden."

"Adden was used to working with designers who don't know how to make things," Dunnigan said, "so when they would tell us that something couldn't be done, we would draw or make them a prototype to show them that it could." Even so, there were certain things for which Adden could not afford to tool up, such as wide, consistent miter joints. It wasn't as if they didn't know how to saw wide miters, since that requires nothing more sophisticated than a sliding table saw; it was that they couldn't guarantee consistent assembly without a big investment in clamps. After intense back-and-forth, "we came up with a faux miter joint—a hybrid bamboo miter joint for the chests and tables," Hurd said. "This was just one of many breakthroughs in which we learned that the whole is greater than the sum of its parts."

The table top, made of environmentally sustainable bamboo plywood, wraps over the end in a deep rebate that not only suggests a tablecloth but also replaces the end apron, simplifying construction and helping hold down costs. The furniture suite uses the same simple side chair for studying and dining; the line also includes a tall stool and a counter-height worktable (not shown).

The "faux miter" Hurd refers to is a deep rebate made possible by the team having selected one of the many new bamboo-based sheet materials now available. In its own Southeast Asian habitat, bamboo is an exceedingly dense and tenacious plant that grows rapidly, so sustainable plantations are not difficult to manage. Structurally, the $7/8$-inch bamboo ply that DEZCO chose resembles old-fashioned blockboard—the top and bottom plies are about $1/8$-inch thick, made of edge-glued bamboo strips about an inch wide, while the core consists of uniform bamboo slats standing on edge. The resulting board is hard, flat, and stable, with no internal voids, so it needs no edge band. That alone makes for major cost savings, while also satisfying DEZCO's requirement for materials honesty: what you see and touch is what it is.

In addition to honesty, the designers were after flexibility. Consider the bed design: knowing that some students like raised beds to allow for

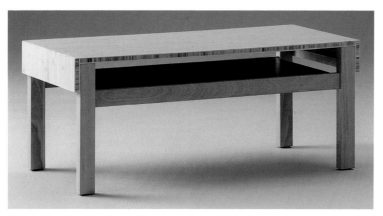

The low coffee table, made of the same eco-friendly bamboo plywood and European beech as the other pieces in the line, features the deep-rebate end apron. Since dorm rooms are chronically short on space and long on stuff, it also provides a broad shelf underneath.

storage underneath and others prefer low ones that function like couches, DEZCO wanted to address both needs while abiding by Residence Life's admonition against visibly adjustable hardware. To complicate matters further, the beds had to fit existing 84-inch alcoves in the converted residence building, and with standard 80-inch mattresses, there was simply no room for conventional head- and footboards. While they puzzled over this central piece in the line, Somerson found herself blurting out: "If we can just get the bed, the rest will follow." Of course, that proved true in both senses once they zeroed in on a modified four-post frame that, oriented one way, puts the mattress at 18 inches above the floor, or flipped over, raises it up to 36 inches. This strategy required a cross-rail at the head and foot, a design feature the team chose to echo throughout the line.

Flexibility was also important in DEZCO's own approach to the process. When their original chair design, which featured a laminated seat and back

on a beech understructure, came in just under $100, they were disheartened that it was $30 over budget. But the team responded by analyzing Adden's existing chairs and production capabilities, and submitted a revised design that relied on what the manufacturer already knew how to do. This resulted in a chair that cost $8 under budget. In the process, they produced a more ergonomically sound chair by using a standard seat curve but flipping the normally concave panel over, yielding a convex seat that "encourages you to sit upright," Somerson explained. The chair has extra rails under the seat for book or laptop storage, which not coincidentally adds considerable strength, as does the back rail at floor level. "Students can be tough on chairs," Dunnigan observed.

As for their green goals, Sage incorporates a plywood made of bamboo harvested from a managed forest in China, along with a new type of MDF made with non-toxic binders that does not need edge-banding. "A lot of companies use glues and formaldehyde and then seal them with edging," Somerson explained, "but we were emphatic about the truthfulness of the materials we used, so we found an MDF that doesn't have to be sealed up to be safe." It is also "stronger and more durable than traditional MDF," Dunnigan pointed out, and the color permeates the material so that scratches are less likely to show.

If the line was to be marketed as environmentally smart, the claims made by the various materials had to be verifiably true. The bamboo plywood was key, but the choice of beech for the solid-wood legs and rails, from a sustainably managed forest in Slovenia, was equally important and required a similar amount of research. "What we liked about the beech was its color, which looked great alongside the bamboo, and its quiet, uniform grain, which made it consistently reliable to machine," Dunnigan said. But even that required negotiations with Adden. "We modeled thinner legs, but Adden had to have a 2-inch dimension for their 32-millimeter joining equipment," he explained.

The designers chose rubber for the drawer pulls because it's a natural material that feels good to the touch, and went with 100% recycled polyester fabric for the soft seating designs—an upholstered chair and two- and three-seat sofas that can be combined in different ways—that were manufactured by Bergeron Enterprises in Assonet, MA. The upholstery fabric is "touted as one of the greenest lines commercially available," Dunnigan explained, "but stands up to all the criteria for number of rubs and durability."

Marketing more widely

As a result of this collaboration, Adden is "creating a new market category to respond to growing institutional interest in sustainability," Hurd said. The company has begun promoting the new brand as "A Rhode Island School of Design and Adden Furniture Evergreen Collaboration" and is describing it with the catch-phrase "virescent furniture—for living and meeting."

In the end, RISD, DEZCO, and Adden are pleased with the outcome—with preserving the soul of the original designs while acknowledging the realities of making "thousands of $220 desks as opposed to one $22,000 piece," as Hurd put it. RISD students, the end-users for the first production run, are also pleased; they find the pieces to be comfortable, functional, and aesthetically appealing without competing with their own style. And they are especially appreciative of the effort these three faculty designers—two of whom also graduated from RISD—made to respond to their needs.

"One of the really interesting aspects of this project is that we were designing furniture for the students themselves, so it makes for a particularly relevant teaching tool," Somerson said. "Because of the complexity of the design stages, we are able to use it as an example that offers concrete specifics

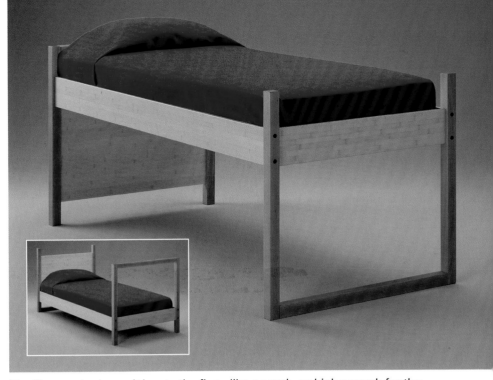

The flip-over bed can sit low to the floor, like a couch, or high enough for the three-drawer bureaus to slide underneath. Its flat and smooth platform allows students to store drawings or press clothes under the lightweight mattress. The suite also includes a double bed (not shown).

to model the design process." Walker concurred: "I have brought this project into the professional practices studio I teach to seniors because it gives them contact with the industry in a real sense and I am able to use it to take them through the entire process."

For the studio furniture makers/designers/professors who took as much of a professional risk with this project as RISD did, the rewards are many. "I discovered the pleasure of good collaboration," Somerson said, explaining that she had always resisted designing as part of a team since her own work is "so personal." Walker is gratified that traditional manufacturers are showing "a genuine commitment to investing in green aspects of design," while Dunnigan pointed to the value of re-learning a classic lesson: "That to design something really simple is difficult." All in all, the three agreed that "going through this many redesigns and refinements helps you really get to the essence of your design," as Somerson summed up. "It often seems like you start with the essence, but in a project like this, it's largely where you end up."

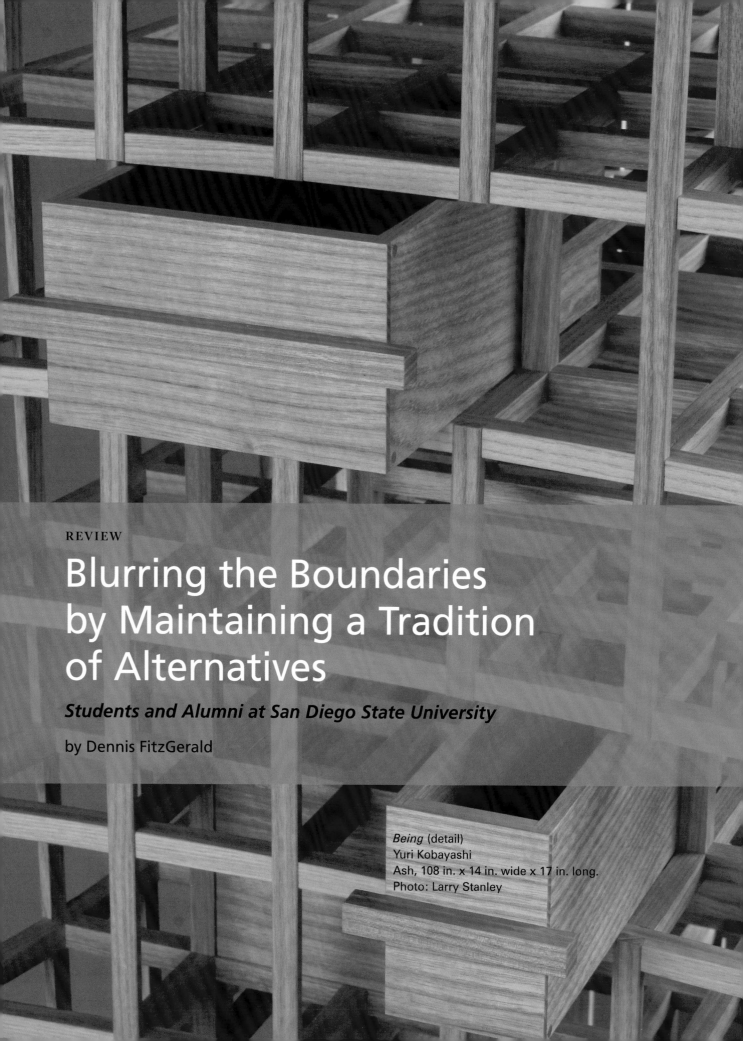

REVIEW

Blurring the Boundaries by Maintaining a Tradition of Alternatives

Students and Alumni at San Diego State University

by Dennis FitzGerald

Being (detail)
Yuri Kobayashi
Ash, 108 in. x 14 in. wide x 17 in. long.
Photo: Larry Stanley

Student and alumni exhibits are not generally concise or unified. They tend to be the opposite, expressing divergent paths and presenting very distinct junctures in individual careers. On one level this held true at San Diego State University. The exhibit, entitled "The Maruyama School: Maintaining a Tradition of Alternatives," spread out between two completely separate rooms displaying a wide range of furniture pieces in no particular order. There was an exorbitant number of wall pieces, with the freestanding work sometimes on platforms or elsewhere placed directly on the floor as furniture in use. In spite of these inconsistencies, the exhibit was pleasantly presented with adequate space for viewing, achieving a continuity that accurately reflected the SDSU program.

One aspect of this exhibit resounded: The presence of Wendy Maruyama. The catalog title, *The Maruyama School*, was not in jest. Maruyama has been the principle teacher and mentor for all of the artists in this exhibit. For an example of Maruyama's own work, see page 39.

Educators who are also professional artists often avoid exposing their students to their own work for fear that they will be unduly influenced. In Maruyama's case, this would be almost impossible.

This is not to say that she relies on showing her own work in the classroom, only that the magnitude of her body of work is unavoidable and an important factor in what attracts students to SDSU in the first place. Whether or not a teacher showcases his or her own work, its philosophical underpinnings almost always becomes the mainstay of the teaching. Maruyama's work has evolved over the years but there has been a constant that clearly drives her both as an artist and educator: her relentless curiosity, along with her determination to challenge and understand herself and the world around her. This is what Maruyama has always brought to the classroom, and this attitude also characterizes, even identifies, her students' work.[1]

There is one other pertinent characteristic that Maruyama brings to the classroom: her passion. Reflecting on her own beginnings, she offers, "You know, feeling that strange sort of flush that gets your heartbeat up, and opens up your mind to something that really, truly triggers a desire to discover more; finding a path that one feels so comfortable with and continuing that pursuit of happiness."[2] Perhaps this is what truly makes a great teacher: the ability to recognize and to pass along one's own enthusiasm.

The annual Furniture Society conferences provide attendees with a richness of visual and conceptual delights, not least of which are the many concurrent exhibitions. The 2005 conference, "The Other Side: A Tradition of Alternatives," hosted in partnership with San Diego State University (SDSU), offered a wide range of exhibits both on campus and off. These ranged from an international exhibit, "Convergence," to a domestic study, "Roy McMakin: A Slat-Back Chair," to the newest annual event, "Faculty Selects," to the impromptu "Members Gallery." A highlight of the 2005 conference exhibitions was a showing of recent work by SDSU students and alumni, titled appropriately, "The Maruyama School: Maintaining a Tradition of Alternatives."

In assembling these conferences the Furniture Society has a number of reasons for partnering with institutions that have studio furniture programs. These collaborations enable the conferences to be presented in very different geographic areas and to a large degree the conference programming reflects the uniqueness of these areas. It affords the opportunity for these institutions to strut their stuff so members may taste what's unique about a particular area or university program, and, as in the case of this exhibition, it provides links to the compelling underpinnings of the work produced by students and alumni.

This was primarily an alumni exhibit. Of the 26 pieces, six were by current students and two by the current artist-in-residence. A call for entries was prepared and distributed by several alumni. All entries were juried by Wendy Maruyama, long-time head of the SDSU furniture program. The prospectus sought work completed after January 2003 and asked that it address the conference theme, "The Other Side: A Tradition of Alternatives." Accepted work was to be shipped at the artist's expense, the exhibit was mounted by the participants, and a modest catalog was put together at the last minute.

—Dennis FitzGerald

Dennis FitzGerald is coordinator of the woodworking and furniture program at State University of New York, Purchase, a past president of The Furniture Society, and a member of the Furniture Studio editorial advisory board.

The work in this exhibition was deeply grounded, fresh, reverent, exploratory, and diverse. Maruyama clearly delights in her students. She writes, "Our program has developed a reputation for creating renegade explorers, melding tradition with alternative and often unorthodox methods of work, and for crossing over disciplines."[3]

The accompanying catalog included a brief statement from most of the artists. In some cases these were generalized artist statements, while others spoke to the particular piece on display. In each case the emphasis was clearly on the artist's intentions and expectations. The work presented here was predominantly about individual exploration, sometimes deeply personal, sometimes a reflection of the cultural/social influences on the artist, sometimes combined with concerns about formal elements, sometimes in response to traditional furniture—but always true to Maruyama's message, to explore and question.

Against the Wall

When we think of furniture, usually we visualize chairs, table and casegoods, all freestanding objects that might use a wall architecturally in their placement but do not mount on or otherwise rely on the wall structurally. Of the 26 pieces exhibited, half were either wall-mounted or used the verticality of the wall, with four of them—by Adrian French, Duncan Gowdy, Mia Hall, and Matt Hutton—relying on a single leg making contact with the floor, with the wall to provide the support that otherwise would have required additional legs. French's "table" is a transforming piece that in one state is a wall sculpture, then when transformed into its alternate state becomes a low table. In each case the traditional mobility of table or casegood has been eliminated, not only tying the pieces to architectural structures but also presenting them as objects on display, challenging the more traditional role of furniture.

Tabled (2004)
Adrian French
Birch, maple,
anodized aluminum;
closed, 92 in. high x 8 in. wide
x 6.5 in. deep;
open, 92 in. high x 34 in. wide
x 58 in. deep.
Photo: Adrian French

French writes that this piece "focuses on elaborate object interaction. Through a series of actions a vertical architectural post transforms into a modern low-lying table for four or five people to dine at in a kneeling fashion. Through contemplation of this object and its interactions, I hope the user will begin to see the complex, nearly ritualistic relationships they have with many objects."

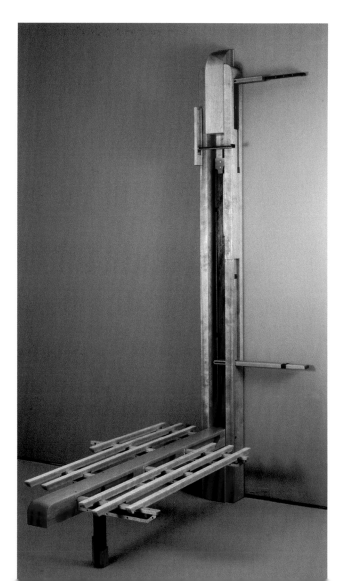

The remaining nine wall pieces (ten if you count Jennifer Anderson's alternate chair covers mounted on the wall as Shaker-like chairs) retain some element of functionality (shelf, drawers, doors), but seemed to be more about the object as repository for the expression of the artist with function reduced to a reference, if not to irrelevance.[4] One repeated activity of these pieces, including an ingenious cabinet by Maruyama herself featuring a sliding panel that exposed two different photographs, is to use them as studies of self by presenting the external while suggesting or inviting exploration of the internal through such aids as cutouts and slides.[5] In these instances, the furniture's use is to be a metaphor. Mounting these objects on the wall at viewer height encourages personal study in much the way we might explore a painting. It invites the viewer to discover the artist's emotive state or, as in the case of Christine Enos's mirror with drop-down coat hooks, the viewer's own.

below: The Unmentionables II & III (2004)
Mia Hall
Wenge, plywood, steel, mixed media;
26 in. high x 24 in. wide x 19 in. deep.
Photo: Larry Stanley

Hall writes, "The two bedside tables are part of a series dealing with issues and concerns around the topic of female sexuality…the left bedside table contains objects intended for female sexual self-gratification and the drawer on the right table holds an assortment of condoms. All three pieces in the series are intended for a strong, independent woman requesting sexual equality…"

below: Croze (2005)
Duncan Gowdy
Maple, brass; 45 in. high x 31 in. wide x 16 in. deep.
Photo: Dean Powell

"A diverse New England family history is the base of my objects. Croze was inspired by a cooper's croze, used on whaling ships to the croze to mark inner sections of the barrels. The original is fabricated from whale bone."

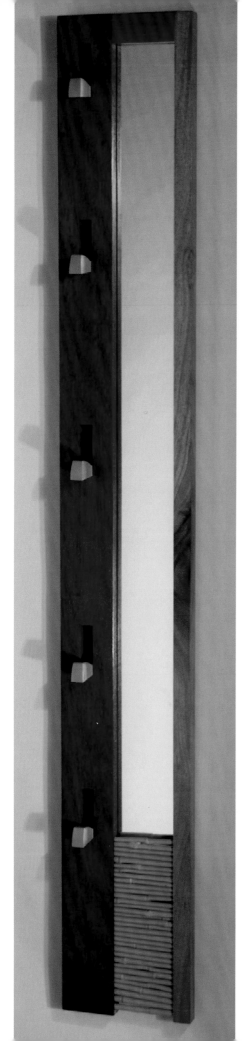

left: Blue Bamboo (2004)
Christine Enos
Mahogany, bamboo, mirror, paint;
52 in. high x 7 in. wide x 2 in. deep.
Photo: Larry Stanley

The blue protrusions are coat, hat, or towel hangers that fold up and all drop down when the user toggles any one of them. Enos writes, "I like to apply the interaction that takes place between an object and the viewer as a metaphor for the interaction that goes on between individuals."

below: Core Sample (2005)
Matt Hutton
Mahogany, fiberglass, hydrocal;
39 in. high x 12 in. dia.
Photo: Jay York

Hutton writes, "I have been using the title 'core sample' to describe a number of recent pieces…that possess fossil-like qualities."

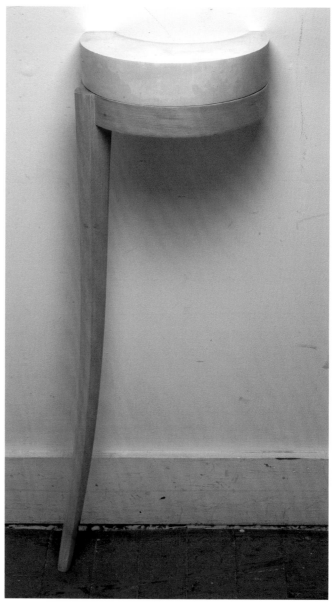

Cutouts that Entice

These explorations are certainly not limited to wall-mounted objects. Heather McCalla's floor cabinet also uses cutouts, enticing the viewer with glimpses of the contrast between exterior and interior. Christine Lee leaves a corner of her steel structure open for the viewer to see the recycled phone books that—presumably—fill the core, contrasting the hardness of the metal with paper, suggesting exploration of environmental issues and social structure. Yuri Kobayashi has created a sensuously exquisite frame structure that refers to the body. The skin removed, we are directly invited, via the inclusion of little drawers, to examine the interior compartments of one's own inner self. Lynn Szymanski's cabinets, a series of small casegood pieces representing homes, invite the viewer through glass doors to discover the objects placed within, an invitation not completely transparent as she has also incorporated secret drawers under the cabinets.

Untitled (cabinet) (2005)
Heather McCalla
Plywood, poplar, mahogany, paint,
embroidery floss;
77 in. high. x 18 in. wide,
x 14 in. deep.
Photo: Larry Stanley

McCalla writes, "My work thus far has been focused on methodology and technical mastery. Now that I am confident in my technical skills I have begun to move away from this practical design approach and I am investigating additional creative possibilities."

above, with detail at left:
Folded Creased Stacked (2004)
Christine Lee
Recycled phonebooks, steel;
35 in. high x 12 in. wide x 90 in. long.
Photo: Larry Stanley

Lee writes, "Combining my obsessive/compulsive nature with my interest in recycled materials leads me to construct objects that question the necessity of traditional materials and function…I interpret the function of furniture as constantly evolving in response to questions of the present day. I want to engage the viewer in both contemplative and physical space."

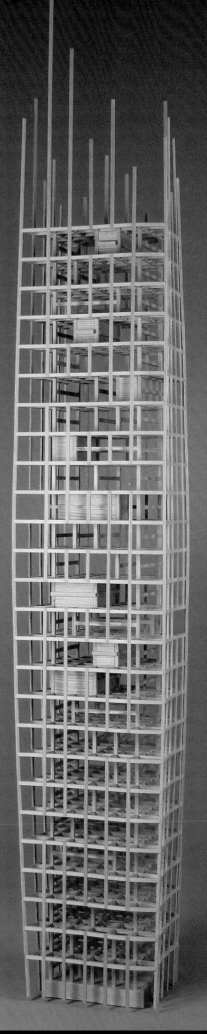

Being (2005)
Yuri Kobayashi
Ash; 108 in. x 14 in. wide x 17 in. long.
Photo: Larry Stanley

Kobayashi writes, "This piece speaks
of the complexity of human nature.
It expresses both the physical and mental
body, which is amazingly strong, yet
surprisingly weak. Memories, feelings
and experiences are our intangible and
intellectual belongings, characterizing
our personality. The drawers symbolize
those intangibles."

Formal Explorations

Exploration was also formal. Dave Fobes's *Twelve-Sided Table* is a study of form and repetition. It presents an interesting positive/negative that explores the ambiguity of opposites juxtaposed with his fascination of the number 12. Srdjan Simic's glass and steel table explores the purity of geometric form, challenging the viewer's perception via the cantilevering of offset elements. Barbara Holmes's table explores the uncommon use of material (sonoboard) in a strikingly simple knock-down table that relies on color to create contrast. This table was unique to this show as the only piece designed for production.

Twelve-Sided Tables (2003)
David Fobes
Laminated oak, ply, paint; 24 in. high x 24 in. dia.
Photo: David Fobes

Writes Fobes, "The coopering has been reversed to yield a mating relationship of the adjacent faces. These are really inverse twins, yielding to each other's demands for physical and psychological space in a shared amniotic environment."

Challenging

Overall, this body of work demonstrated an expansive use of materials, often challenging fixed notions and methods. I found the work presented to be exquisite, full of meaning and rich in dialog. It challenges one to examine the influences and culture that affects and drives our creative processes and ultimately our lives. This exhibit represents a new generation that is indebted to Wendy Maruyama, the artist and the teacher. Ever the rebel, always challenging, yet also nurturing. Her students have embraced her legacy.

What may be the most challenging point of continued discussion is how this exhibit represents the field of studio furniture and its direction in the 21st century. The driving force behind this work (and—if this exhibit is indicative—of all Maruyama's students) is not merely to explore but to do so particularly at the boundaries of studio furniture. These artists are approaching furniture as a medium of self-expression.[6] It could be said that this work is more about the "art" of furniture than about the "design" of furniture. Or perhaps, this exhibit is more about "art" than about "furniture."

I would further offer that this exhibit most curiously represents the deconstruction of labels as to where objects fit most precisely within traditional notions about fine art, craft, and design. From a material point of view, furniture programs have evolved in the last 20 years from being almost completely tied to woodworking processes to embracing all and any available material. This exhibit demonstrated the fact of this changeover. This is clearly a positive development, as it rejects categorizing studio furniture as an activity based in a single medium. Might this also be true with how we categorize object making? In his essay "Craft as Art," John Perreault supports this expanded notion: "...what I call usable art—not quite craft, not quite design, but something else: sculpture that has function."[7] He refers to Scott Burton's work as furniture/sculpture[8] and artists like Judy Chicago who appropriate furniture forms in their work. Might the furniture in this exhibit be better understood in this broader context?

To blur traditional boundaries in pursuit of a new perspective does have its consequences. In his essay on the evolution of American Craft, Bob Barnard (in a slightly different context) quotes Peter Plagens's perspective: "A big problem with sculpture these days is that practically anything can call itself sculpture...It is a form increasingly bereft on a convincing convention."[9] Does studio furniture benefit from a blurring of its boundaries? If so, how might this body of work further define the art of furniture making?

Notes

1. For backround see review by Lisa Hammel in *American Craft*, Feb./March 1993.

2. Catalog for *The Maruyama School: Maintaining a Tradition of Alternatives*, June 8-11, 2005, designed by Kirby Jones.

3. Ibid.

4. Ibid. See statements in the catalog.

5. See review by Lisa Hammel in *American Craft* Feb./March 1993.

6. See *Furniture Studio 3*, Baldon: "Emerging Artists Confront Traditional Notions About Function and Craft").

7. *Objects and Meaning*, edited by M. Anne Fariello and Paula Owens, page 79.

8. See review of *Design ≠ Art* by John J. Curley in *Furniture Studio 3*.

9. *Objects and Meaning*, edited by M. Anne Fariello and Paula Owens, page 56.

Early Green and Baby Blue (2005)
Barbara Holmes
SONOboard, MDF, paint;
18 in. high x 18 in. wide x 28 in. long.
Photo: Barbara Holmes

Holmes writes, "This small storage stool/table comes together using slotted panel construction for ease in assembly and disassembly. The panels are colored on both sides, giving the stool a dual tone that can be changed simply by pulling the panels apart and reversing them."

Stepped Coffee Table (2005)
Srdjan Simic
Steel frame, patina, clear coat, clear glass;
36 in. wide x 36 in. deep x 18 in. high.
Photo: Srdjan Simic

Srdjan Simic emigrated from Yugoslavia in 1996, with a background in graphic design and architecture.

Hitting the Design Wall, and Climbing Over

How a mid-career artist gave up glue and got back in touch with her own work

by Gail Fredell

detail from *Silver Lake, entry table,* p. 60

Making furniture is a pursuit often fraught with mishaps and challenges as well as accomplishments and successes. Difficulties arise from technical unknowns, engineering problems, uncooperative materials and weather, equipment failures or lack thereof, demanding schedules, less than bountiful budgets. Obstacles also present themselves in human form as clients, subcontractors, architects, and decorators.

The most daunting challenge, the design wall, is not the result of outside issues but a manifestation of conflict within myself. It comes up when

I reach a place where I no longer relate to what I am making, how or why I am making it. It doesn't matter that my furniture may be commissioned, exhibited, published, or collected. Encouraging and supportive as these accomplishments might be, they cannot convince me that my work is okay if in my heart I know it's just not cutting it. Like James Joyce's Mr. Duffy, who "lived a short distance from his body," my work is in one place and I'm somewhere else, which is where I found myself a couple of summers ago.

I had completed an unusually large and long commission and received both gratitude from my clients and praise from a wider public. Though satisfied in many ways with the project, at gut level I felt unfulfilled. I began to question my motivations, designs, and fabrication processes, as well as my ability to evaluate my own work. I wanted to sell my tools, equipment, and materials, and just walk away. I longed do something else and to feel differently.

Gail Fredell

Around this time I had the opportunity and good fortune to attend a workshop led by Pema Chodron at Naropa Institute in Boulder, CO. Her many excellent books on Tibetan Buddhist teachings and practice had formed the core of my evening readings for months. Pema writes extensively on Tonglen practice and its accompanying Lojong slogans, offering a contemporary view and personal interpretation of their ancient wisdom. One slogan in particular provided the point of departure for my adventure ahead:

"Of the two views, hold the principal one." She explains: "You're the only one who knows. One kind of witness is everybody else giving you his or her feedback or opinions. This is worth listening to; there's some truth in what people say. The principal witness, however, is you. You're the only one who knows when you're opening and when you're closing. You're the only one who knows when you're

using things to protect yourself and keep your ego together and when you're opening and letting things fall apart; letting the world come in as it is— working with rather than struggling against it. You're the only one."

This advice gave me permission to honor my doubts, to question my methods of work, evaluate my designs, and look for a way to reconnect with what I was doing with my furniture. Disconcerting as it was to find myself facing the design wall again, the good news was that I could see it. Once I acknowledged where I was and what I was looking at there was no turning back, or in this case, no standing still. Not if I wanted to be at peace again with my work. The search was on. As Pema wrote, "The search is what everyone would undertake were he not stuck in the everydayness of his or her own life. To be aware of the search is to be on to something. Not to be on to something is to be in despair."

How many of us, when faced with the design wall, look outside ourselves, beyond our own experience, for answers to questions or design problems? How often do we turn to books or magazines, studying work from other lands or countries, expecting or hoping to see our new aesthetic jump off the page? How many of us have fallen into making art derived not from within but derivative of the work of others? When does inspiration settle for imitation?

None of us works in a vacuum, though it can feel that way at times. It is human nature and an undeniable part of the creative process to be inspired by the natural and man-made world

Editor's note—When Gail Fredell presented a longer version of this account at the 2005 Furniture Society conference in San Diego, many in the audience said it was the most moving presentation they had seen. I was there and that was true, but there is more to it than emotion. Fredell, a seasoned maker and teacher, has her finger on a problem that affects many, if not most, mature artists: one day you wake up and find that you don't like, and might not even recognize, your own work. The usual advice is to go do something else for a while.

As in much of her life and career, Fredell chose not to follow that conventional wisdom. Instead of taking a holiday from her work, she threw herself into it. But she

decided to change the rules, giving up on four essential aspects of her craft: gluing, sanding, painting, and measuring. During her conference presentation, I thought that these technical interventions would be the key to her new landscape. But as she makes clear in this essay, these changes, although helpful, were not the key. The real key turned out to be her initial decision, before she got down to technical tinkering, to let go of old habits and ways of thinking and working, to trust herself and her own intuition.

Gail Fredell trained initially as an architect, then entered the graduate furniture program at Rochester Institute of Technology. Today she lives in Basalt, CO.

—John Kelsey

around us—as well as by our artistic heritage and the traditions of our craft. But if we rest in the relative comfort of imitating the work of our contemporaries or of artists from past or distant cultures, we will never discover who, in we are today.

I have a small collection of books well worn from repeated use. Not one is about furniture. They are books on architecture, sculpture, landscape, and Zen. There is a certain comfort in referencing them, like calling up a close friend when in a place of doubt or fear. But sometimes not even those tried and true resources or companions can open things up when I'm shut down.

Our individual, unique life experiences inform our artwork as much as they form our character and color our point of view. Those experiences define our perception of ourselves, our relationships with others, and influence our approach to our work. They inspire our visual vocabulary, determine our work ethic, and serve as the foundation of our aesthetic. For reasons unknown, it occurred to me to tap into the other-than-work areas of my life (there actually were a couple) to look for information to apply to the problem I was facing in the studio with my work. Maybe, just maybe, there was some wisdom inherent in or resulting from my recent life experiences. I had, after all, had some positive and successful ones in the face of admittedly daunting circumstances.

Since August of 2001 I have maintained a workshop in the Aspen area, working full-time as a studio furniture artist. I returned to the studio after an eight-year tenure at Anderson Ranch as the director of the Furniture and Wood Turning Programs. I was out of practice as a maker, lacking momentum as a designer, devoid of self-confidence. I was a beginner all over again. It has taken four-plus years to get back up to speed. Just in the past year I have had moments where the designs are flowing and there is a lightness and economy at work. Most of the time it has been a real struggle. But I have had enough glimpses to keep me going.

During that time I also recovered from a long-running, life-threatening bout with alcoholism. Despair is not unfamiliar. The early stages of my recovery were based in AA, the fellowship and program of Alcoholics Anonymous. More recently my recovery has been supported by my study of Buddhist teachings, my return to a long-abandoned sitting meditation practice.

My experience in AA and on my cushion provided me immeasurable and invaluable guidance through the perils of addiction to the rewards of recovery. The people I encountered along the way, the fellowship, my sangha, and my family saved my life. It was to the lessons of recovery and to Buddhist teachings and practice that I turned in search of clues as to how to proceed through my dilemma at work. Both the *Big Book of Alcoholics Anonymous* and Buddhist writings abound with slogans intended to encourage and wake one up along the path. Study or stare at them long enough and they just sort of slip into your consciousness at the most opportune times. Several of these short phrases provided exactly what I needed: encouragement to let go and move toward the uncertainty of change.

My favorite quote from AA is the definition of insanity: "Doing the same thing over and over, expecting different results." For anyone familiar with addiction, relapse prevention, and recovery, this definition needs no further clarification. It is complemented by the statement: "If you want to get and stay sober, you only have to change one thing: everything." In *Start Where You Are,* Pema Chodron explains that the Lojong teachings present the possibility of "an entire change of attitude." She continues: "'Train in the three difficulties' is my favorite slogan because it acknowledges that this path is difficult, all right, but it is a good way to spend your time. The first is seeing neurosis as neurosis, and the second is being willing to do something about it. The third difficulty is the aspiration to make this a way of life."

A slogan that goes along with the first difficulty, seeing neurosis as neurosis, says, "Liberate yourself by examining and analyzing." Since there is room for neither insanity nor neurosis in my recovery or life, and as liberation sounded very appealing, I set out to follow the advice to examine, analyze, and change.

Looking Back

To begin the process I took a look not only at my recent work but at the whole picture of what I had been doing over time. In one evening I went through drawers, files, and binders of photos of everything I had made over the last 30 years. I arrived at small but cohesive body of work which, although made in the past, continued to hold meaning for me that day. Without exception, these projects were done not as commissions but speculatively for gallery and museum exhibitions. All, with one exception, were landscape-inspired. All had sold quickly. Three had landed in museums.

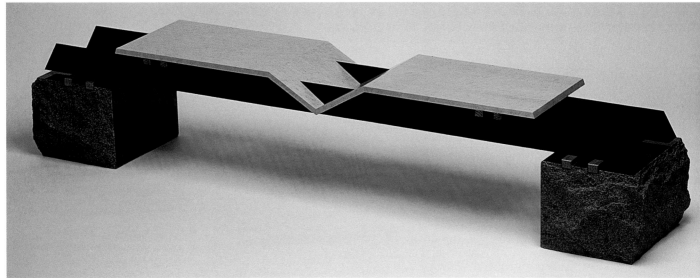

top: Entry Table (1985)
Cherry, steel.

"Mountain valley and water."

above: Donner Pass, bench (1989)
Granite, steel, bird's-eye maple.

"Snow sheds that cover train tracks over Donner Pass in the Sierras."

right: 110° in the Shade, bench (1987)
Granite, ebonized mahogany, aluminum rods, patinated bronze.

"A singular, cool, restful place at the end of a long day's hike."

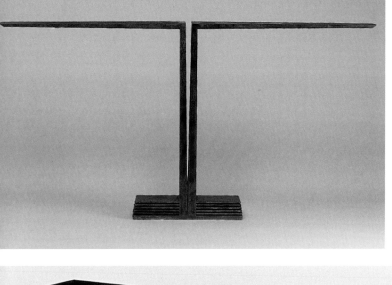

above: Graphite to Taste,
rocker (1989)
Diamond plate steel.

Perimeter line, two
incisions, four folds, rocker.

above, left:
Canyonlands,
entry table (1990)
Patinated steel.

"Zion National Park, looking
up to the sky from deep in
the canyons."

left: Silver Lake,
entry table (1989)
Wenge, patinated bronze.

"Low lake bed in the
Sierras during the 1980s
California drought."

right: October Stream (1990)
Granite bench, painted OSB floor, aluminum river and reservoir, 1/8-inch dowel forest.

Bench by Gail Fredell. Installation in collaboration with William Peters, landscape architect.

"A path through grasses to a comfortable place to rest. In the spirit of the raked sand and stone Zen gardens, it refers to a greater landscape of mountain, reservoir, stream, and forest."

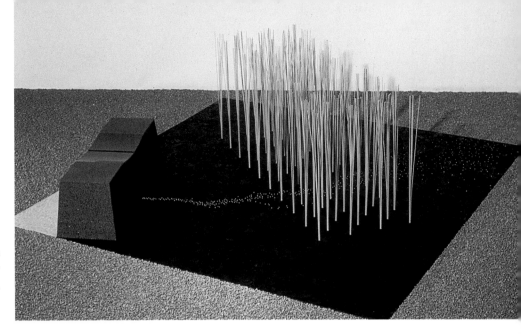

left: Dark Sky Night, entry table (1990)
Ebonized cherry.

"A slice of the Pacific Ocean meeting the land on a dark sky night."

below: Red Road, buffet table (2002)
Pearwood, painted spruce, steel, climbing rope wrap.

"Road of recovery."

Taking this overview and seeing the parallels among my favorite projects convinced me to do something I hadn't done for more than 15 years: make my own work. I had no preconceived notions of where I wanted to go with my aesthetic. What I did have was a somewhat surprising amount of trust in my decision to go for it without actually knowing what "it" was. I had a willingness to let go, to change my habitual patterns, to trust in the process as it evolved, and to proceed without attachment to the outcome. I also gave myself the freedom to fail, not typically an option when working for clients.

The decision to set commissions aside was easy to make. The next step was to bring the examining and analyzing process into the present and to take an honest look at how I was working, as I searched for clues for a future aesthetic direction.

I suspected that the lengthy time span of my recent projects was contributing to my malaise, as was the process of working on commissions. When doing these projects my usual sequence is: design, present the design, get approval, make the deposit, and build as designed/approved. I felt that this measured way of working was contributing to my separateness from both my shop work and my completed projects. There was scant room for working intuitively or spontaneously. I set out to work as directly as possible, to work without sketches, models, samples, working drawings, or estimates, and made a commitment to completing and entry hall table and a bench in four weeks.

The cost, preciousness, and in some cases the weight of materials involved on recent commissions had been daunting to say the least. I had, out of necessity, taken to moving components around in my shop with an engine hoist. The cost-of-goods-sold, that is the total of materials and subcontractors' work, was ranging from 20% to 30% of project budgets. I had recently discovered a source for recycled/reclaimed lumber and decided that the table and bench would be built entirely of this material and that any metal components would be fabricated simply out of steel.

I felt a longing not only to redefine my aesthetic but also to rediscover the simple pleasure of making stuff. When I bought my first Japanese

chisels in 1974, it was not a purchase based on aspirations for a career as a studio furniture artist, but one motivated by the simple desire to work with my hands, fine tools, and with wood, something I had always enjoyed doing, especially with my father. There was probably a bit of rejection of architecture in there, too. In 30 years of making furniture I had carved out a sort of technological comfort zone for myself, using the same processes over and over. I questioned whether my designs were driving my methods of work or if those practiced and familiar methods were defining and limiting my aesthetic. So while I was letting go of predictable design methodologies I tossed some of my most dependable fabrication process. I swore off paint, sanding, glue and, best of all, measuring. In doing so I opened the doors to a more articulated and direct visual vocabulary.

The easiest to give up was paint. I had never felt particularly talented or skilled with a brush or pigment, especially in light of the work of Gary Knox Bennett, who worked down the street, or of Wendy Maruyama, Kim Kelzer, and Fabianne Garcia, all of whom shared my workshop during the 1980s. The basis of my new palette would be natural oils, dyes, and tannic-acid reactive pickles that would enhance and react with the wood instead of obscuring it.

Surfaces sanded to 320-grit gave way to hand-scraped and hand-planed ones. Marks resulting from joinery and the shaping process were simply a result of the construction process and visually honest. But it soon became evident that if my hand-work was to be revealed on my completed project I had better tune up my tools and hone my skills. I have since had the opportunity to study Japanese design and woodworking with Osamu Shoji in a summer workshop at Anderson Ranch. Shoji-san's course was as inspiring as it was instructional, and to this day contributes immeasurably to my sense of well-being in the studio and to the well-being of my planes and chisels.

Making furniture had become as much about glue-ups as about woodworking. Metal components and details had long been a part of my visual vocabulary but were not always structurally necessary or honest.

John Wayne, Jr., hall table, 2004
Spruce, redwood, steel

"Portrait of my father."

I made the decision to work without glue, using gravity and mechanical connections in as honest and direct a manner as possible.

The most liberating gesture in this process of letting go was to just put my measuring tapes away in a drawer. Instead of predetermining measurements by numbers, dimensions were discovered by experience and proportions refined by eye. I just worked directly with components during fabrication until they looked right. Even steel components that were to be cut with a CAD-operated plasma cutter were mocked-up first, then measured for my fabricator.

Here's the new work

On occasion, I have made small tables that have been portraits. I had done my Mom, and always wanted to do a portrait of my Dad, affectionately known in our family as John Wayne, Jr. This table follows a structural format I have been pursuing for the past four years. The table legs and top are connected through a core steel box; it bolts together with two wrenches. While this piece is not exactly landscape-inspired, it does feature bold timbers of spruce. I was dangerously close to log furniture but I hoped the table legs would look like chaps and the top would look like the wide brim of my father's hat. Solid, straightforward, strong.

The bench was next. It was, as with JW Jr., constructed entirely of recycled lumber. These materials are challenging. They tend to crack and warp on a daily basis, risking explosion when they go through the machines. The materials themselves required that I loosen up a bit. This bench, like so many I have done, has a bridge-like order to the components: two pylons and a span. Rarely do I incorporate backrests in my bench designs. Yet in this bench the slightly folded backrest was the point of departure for the overall design and for the

Bench (2004)
Redwood, spruce, steel, turquoise, silver leaf

organization of the components. And I did loosen up on my guidelines and introduce glue along the backrest joint.

The bench marked a return to the landscape for visual imagery. The irregular wane edge along the top refers to the mountain rim or horizon one constantly sees from the floor of the valley where I live. The backrest has a front detail of turquoise silver-leaf squares hurling towards a distant lake. I envisioned the bench finding a home near water.

When the table and bench were completed, I felt a sense of accomplishment that had escaped me for years. I wasn't so sure anyone else would appreciate the work, but I didn't care. The continuing lives of these simple pieces have reaffirmed my efforts. I kept the table in my showroom at the studio for months. In June, new clients came to the shop and bought the table. It was Father's Day. The table will go in the entry hall of their new home in Snowmass, and they have commissioned additional projects.

I donated the bench to the annual art auction at Anderson Ranch Arts Center. The couple who purchased the bench placed it on a spacious terrace overlooking a lake and mountains to the west. Two large garden benches have been commissioned for another terrace facing the same view.

Those four weeks flew by. More than once during that time, I deliberately slowed down the pace of construction, just to savor the process and the gift I had given myself of time to work on my own. When my time was up, I had a major commission ahead: a dining table (with leaves) and accompanying chairs for 12. How could I construct a veneered, torsion box table top without glue, or design and fabricate 12 chairs without measuring? Could I proceed with the commission without losing sight of what I had experienced and come to value through making the table and bench?

The dining table was to be my first veneer project, executed with the expert assistance and guidance of my shop partner, Brian Reid. It was also my first go at abstracted, pictorial imagery, employing hundreds of squares of dyed veneers, and well over one hundred glue-ups. For the chair design, the point of departure was the backrest used in the

above: 12 Dining Chairs (2006)
Pickled mahogany and oak, English brown oak,
rolled steel seats with leather upholstery, steel details.

Chairs designed to accompany *Wood Run.*

right: Wood Run, dining table with extending leaves (2006)
Torsion box construction with dyed veneers, pickled oak,
and mahogany trim.

"A pictorial abstraction of the view from Snowmass Mountain."

bench, and the entire design process was executed through a series of full-scale mock-ups.

The act of swearing off glue, paint, sanding, and measuring was the beginning of my month-long design retreat. But the process-specific components of the experiment were secondary to the decision to "hold the principal view." The most significant and lasting lesson I learned was to trust my intuition and pursue an aesthetic true to my nature and values. Only then will the resulting work have the potential to be resolved, honest, and fulfilling.

I returned to one of those well-worn books, *Between Silence and Light: Spirit in the Architecture of Louis I. Kahn,* to confirm my experience.

"Your intuition is your most exacting sense, it is your most reliable sense. It is the most personal sense that a singularity has, and intuition, not knowledge, must be considered your greatest gift." —Louis I. Kahn

Then I got to work. 🪑

Bibliography

Comfortable with Uncertainty, Pema Chodron, Shambhala, Boston 2002

Boundaries, Maya Lin, Simon & Schuster, NY 2000

The Eight Gates of Zen, John Daido Loori, Dharm Communications, Mt. Tremper, NY 1992

The Ocean in the Sand, Mark Holborn, Shambhala, Boulder 1978

The Gift, Lewis Hyde. Random House, NY 1979

Seeing is Forgetting the Name of the Thing One Sees, Lawrence Weschler, University of California Press, Berkeley 1982

Between Silence and Light: Spirit in the Architecture of Louis I. Kahn, John Lobell, Shambhala, Boulder 1979

The Zen of Creativity, John Daido Loori, Dharma Communications, Mt. Tremper, NY 2005

Lead Toward the Future

Furniture instructors present the best work of their students

by Dean Wilson

I've often said to my new students, "We're all on the same path. The big difference is that I'm just a little farther along."

Many paths lead to the work you see here in the second annual Faculty Selects exhibit. It was juried from 35 entries submitted by faculty at 17 institutions. These students work in a variety of learning environments: vocational/technical schools, community colleges, state universities, specialty schools, and private colleges. They choose among degree programs, non-degree programs, undergrad or graduate programs, structured or independent study. All entries were submitted by an instructor, and initiated in a class of 10 weeks or more as a class assignment or sequence of study.

These students are the future of the field. In a few short years, they will be taking on the role of mentor and model, in the classroom, in industry, and by example in galleries and publications.

Chair (2005)
Aimee Pickett
Cherry,
ash veneer,
fiberglass;
66 in. high
x 48 in. long
x 23 in. wide.

Editor's note—*The work shown here was exhibited at the Furniture Society's 2006 conference at Herron School of Art in Indianapolis. It was chosen by a four-person jury from 35 entries, and in a startlingly rapid change, 30 of them arrived as compact disks containing digital photographs, with only five in the previously standard format, sheets of 35mm slides. This made it possible for us to quickly scan the slides and burn all of the entries onto disks. Thus this competition was juried by computer and telephone— the jurors could view and discuss the same images in real time, without having to travel for a face-to-face meeting.*

The jurors were Dennis FitzGerald, coordinator of the furniture program at the State University of New York, Purchase College, and a past president of The Furniture Society; Dean Wilson, professor and head of the furniture program at Minneapolis (MN) College of Art; John Kelsey, editor of Furniture Studio; and Aimee Pickett of Rochester Institute of Technology School for American Crafts, who is the 2005 student representative to the Furniture Society executive board. Being on the jury made Pickett ineligible for the competition, but you can see a chair she recently made above.

—*John Kelsey*

facing page, with detail above:
Roger & Christine (secretary) (2005)
Aaron Heisler
Savannah (GA) College of Art & Design
Aluminum, stainless steel, plywood, silicone, cherry veneer
36 in. x 14 in. x 20 in.
Photo: Aaron Heisler

The desk was one of 12 pieces in Aaron Heisler's thesis body of work, titled "Context," the focus of which was to incorporate uniquely personal interactions into the process of creating furniture items in a way that would mimic private design commissions. The collection of personal interactions would be part cultural anthropology and random selection of design cues.

The process of developing his work involved investigating the cultural make-up of Savannah for design cues which would then be linked to attributes and comments from random individuals across the fabric of Savannah. A random selection of furniture types would provide the form or canvas on which to embed the cues. The body of work would then become as representative and diverse as the community in which it was designed. Aaron was prolific in the venture and the work was truly diverse as well as coherently presented. Aaron was true to the ideals set out in his proposal and the work represented a creative cross section of Savannah.

—*George Perez, instructor*

The chaise lounge designed and constructed by Julian Laffin was an exercise in patience and perseverance. Julian was one of 18 students in the fine furniture program at Camosun College who took up the challenge of designing and manufacturing seating from the indigenous western maple that grows on Vancouver Island. He successfully met the challenge of using a particularly difficult wood for bent lamination work. All of the bending forms for the chaise components were cut using CNC technology. The contours of the chaise were tested and adjusted using mock-ups and trial fittings. Once the desired curve was obtained the forms were then used in a vacuum bag to create the curved pieces.

The assignment also included criteria for specific shipping size requirements. To achieve this Julian fabricated all of the hardware that is used in the chair, allowing it to be disassembled for shipping. Before any of the student's designs are executed he or she must complete a scale model, a production calendar, and a set of working drawings.

—*Ken Guenter and Cam Russell, instructors*

above: Bent on Maple (2005)
Julian Laffin, Camosun College,
Victoria, BC
Western maple, steel
20 in. x 30 in. x 72 in.
Photo: Ken Guenter

Hayley investigated the spatial opportunities available by simply eroding material away from a rectangular volume to create this visually playful piece. Many interpolations were examined before settling on the angular configuration with the square as a defining element. The opening on the top surface and through the piece is a display feature that allows the user to accessorize in a deliberate and formal way. Hayley was commended for her execution of the complex geometry involved, and the seamless plastic appearance from MDF and painted finish. This is functional piece of sculpture designed and built as part of an introductory furniture studio offered to architecture majors.

—*Leonard Wujcik, instructor*

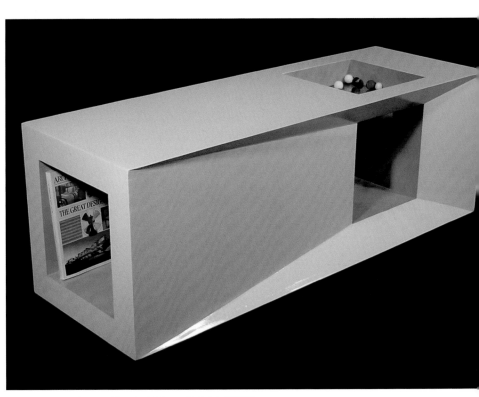

above: Eroded Mass (table) (2005)
Hayley North, University of Kentucky
MDF, glass, paint
18 in. x 18 in. x 54 in.
Photo: Leonard Wujcik

The Passage of Time (storage) (2005)
Yuri Kobayashi
San Diego (CA) State University
Yellow heart, M.D.F., paint
39 in. x 18 in. x 74 in.
Photo: Larry Stanley

Yuri is a third-year MFA student. This piece was completed for her thesis show—there was no specific assignment other than adhering to her proposed theme for her show as described in her artist statement (another piece of similar theme appears on page 53):

"Recently, my interest in creating work is to speak of what I find in everyday life at a universal level, rather than making a piece of furniture. The method I use relates to my personal growth, which is based on disciplines of various kinds. As an athlete, I would run over and over again in training. As an apprentice woodworker, I would perform a single operation for days at a time.... By using repetition in my work, I represent changes in the passage of time or the stream of consciousness."

The concepts of construction and a sense of order, and yet a response to all things natural and organic are symbolized in her work in form, construction, and design. This is a marvelous piece.

—*Wendy Maruyama, professor*

Just Another Bandsaw Box (2004)
Tim Maddox, Kendall College of Art & Design at Ferris State University (MI)
Salvaged pine, steel, paint
40 in. x 18 in. x 18 in.
Photo: Brent Skidmore

Tim was assigned to build a better box. There seemed to be initial budget concerns as he had no money. He proceeded to use some of the most useless-looking yellow pine and began by laminating it and forming bandsaw boxes. My reaction at first was, "Good luck." One, he had chosen an overused technique with many limitations and two, this wood seemed less than forgiving and not promising of anything more worthy than a good doorstop. True to Tim's nature, he set out to turn the ordinary into extraordinary and he did. No, his box couldn't just sit on the floor, it had a beautiful wall mount, and yes, his bandsaw boxes are finely painted and are a new look at a worn-out technique.

—*David Greenwood and Brent Skidmore, instructors*

left: *Rubber Chair* (2005)
Brian Laskowski, Iowa State University, Ames, IA
Copper, rubber, wood
44 in. x 18 in. x 22 in.
Photo: George Ensley

The project was to design a chair form using any material other than wood. My evaluation was that the pieces were well-designed (though there is always room for improvement on craftsmanship). The sense of whimsy and playfulness is good while at the same time they have an erotic side to them. Maybe it's due to the choice of materials, what Brian likes to call "fetish" latex. Overall this is the best work Brian has done and the pieces were true to his original design.

—*Chris Martin, assistant professor*

Jordan has embarked on a series of work that investigates materials and their relationships to one another. With his piece submitted here, he shows in-depth research with the use of ordinary paper and the connections that it can have to furniture. It is work like this that has kept Jordan asking questions and making changes. This is a sure sign of a successful designer/maker.

In addition to being considerate and ambitious, Jordan demonstrates a wide range of skills in the woodworking studio. He understands structure and form well enough to begin to articulate his ideas in the third dimension using furniture techniques. It is rare to find Jordan hindered by a technical difficulty; he is always willing to work through his piece until the end. Jordan's table is refined, well-built, and an excellent result from an investigation of materials.

—*Matt Hutton, assistant professor*

above: Hall Table #1 (2005)
Jordan Gehman, Maine College of Art
Walnut, paper
44 in. x 10 in. x 8 in.
Photo: Matt Hutton

Untitled (chair) (2005)
Jason Calton,
Minneapolis College of Art & Design
Mild steel w/patina
16 in. x 40 in. x 26 in.
Photo: Dean Wilson

The last project for the semester's class, Furniture in Metal, was an open assignment using steel as the main element. Jason's mild-steel chair is constructed as a hollow form, TIG seam-welded, with a chemical patina applied last.

Attention to every detail—whether they be overall design parameters, ergonomic concerns, layout and welding, or finishing—has been worked out with first-class results.

—*Dean Wilson, professor*

Dancing Tables (2004)
Nick Preneta, Northern Michigan University
Maple, epoxy, enamel
42 in. x 30 in. x 14.5 in.
Photo: Nick Preneta

Nick established his own design parameters to incorporate laminate bending, creating a two-part table form that would express a gesture of two people in close proximity to each other.

Nick developed his idea through numerous drawings and models. He experimented with various leg postures and curving tabletop shapes that would fit into one another, creating the sense of a single form. Nick's final solution incorporates a mating concave and convex curve, which meet to form a single shape suggesting yin/yang wholeness. The final position of the legs also suggests the dance-like gesture of a couple in fluid motion. I applaud Nick for this work, as he has carefully integrated the physical and visual aspects to support his intent of expressing the gesture of dancing partners in the utilitarian form of a table.

—*William Leete, professor*

Reproduction Seymour Tambour Secretary (2005)
Andrew McSheffrey
North Bennet Street School (MA)
Mahogany, mahogany and
curly maple veneer
44.75 in. x 37.25 in. x 19.5 in.
Photo: Lance Patterson

Andrew's goals for the project included the tambour, banding, inlay, crossbanding and veneered drawer fronts, cock beading, lopers, spade feet, fold-down desk top, mouldings, experiments with finishes, and working with ivory. He thought he could build it in 14 weeks but it definitely was more than a three-month project. We'd like sto give him some suggestions to help minimize the time without changing it too much.

—*Claire Fruitman, instructor*

Table (2005)
George Dubinsky
Bucks County (PA) Community College
Mahogany, milk paint
25 in. x 20 in. x 20 in.
Photo: Gilbert Browning Studios

A small table is an intimate object with many possibilities of design. In conceptualizing ideas, I try to encourage students to expand the way that they think of the object. George decided to make the legs of his table by turning a large spindle and splitting it into four parts. Additionally, he designed a series of rims that were mostly carved away to produce a series of raised barbs. Producing this illusion required careful technique in the turning and in the carving. The overall design is well-considered and he ended up with a table that fulfilled the assignment with a challenging and unique design.

—*Janice Smith, instructor*

Tuxedo Chair (2004)
Fatie Atkinson
Haywood Community College, NC
Walnut, oak
36 in. x 18 in. x 18 in.
Photo: Fatie Atkinson

The student could choose from five different chair structures that could be used at a desk or dining table. These structures are common to production chair designs. The intent is to not spend time designing the "perfect chair" but to arrive at decisions quickly. Assume you are working within the restrictions of a customer's needs, interests, and budget. The project is as much about the business as it is about how to make a chair. Fatie's solution involved a simple structure that allowed the use of basic mortise-and-tenon joinery. Producing the structure quickly and easily allowed him to embellish the legs with some carving. The seat and backrest are vacuum-formed molded plywood.

As a completed chair the structure proved strong and comfortable. With some minor modifications it could become a production chair, good for producing multiples for a dining set or desk chair. The cost analysis component of the project required an estimate prior to construction and an actual price determined after completion, with consideration for how it could be done more efficiently. The best way to prove if the design and business practice worked is if it would sell. It did— an order was taken for a set in a different wood.

—*Wayne Raab, instructor*

Spalted Cabinet (2005)
Desmond Nault
College of the Redwoods (CA)/Fine Woodworking
Spalted western maple and kwila
55 in. x 20 in. x 12.5 in.
Photo: David Welter

In choosing material for his display cabinet Desmond took a big risk in deciding upon the spalted curly maple for the panels. A little goes a long way. The unconventional asymmetry of the panel pattern is of immediate interest. Then it may be noticed that the asymmetry is carried through the door dimensions. Desmond's intention was to create the feeling of a waterfall with the wood grain of the display surface running counter to the expected side-to-side orientation, running instead from the back, over and down the front. The strong figure of the veneer in the drawer front gives an impression of being horizontal, as would usually be expected, but the pattern is of a piece rather than pieced together.

The overall shape of the cabinet is gentle, with crisp detailing where the post rises above the display surface and in the arc of the top rails. This cabinet meets all of the requirements to be an embraceable object.

—*David Welter, instructor*

Petology (2005)
Rosma Gutierrez
Rhode Island School of Design
Corian, bent ply, leather, foam
48 in. x 12 in. x 12 in.
Photo: Rosma Gutierrez

Students were led through three models for designs focusing on the linear, planar, and volumetric aspects of a chair's design. This method isolates individual design aspects and encourages them to generate more designs before launching into their final choice.

These nesting benches by Rosma Gutierrez connect to a body of work she is developing for her graduate thesis. In Petology (pet*o*lo*gy), Rosma is creating "functional objects that enhance your life" by evoking a comforting emotional response and a sense of well-being that she sees in our relationships with pets. She derives her forms from her selection of "weird South American animals that have a prehistoric quality," such as the alligator, sloth, anteater, platypus, and tapir. These animals have a certain attraction while still being strange and mysterious.

These forms were made from formed Corian and bent plywood in a variety of sizes: mama, papa, and child. In keeping with the material explanation of the project, some forms have elements upholstered in leather. Rosma is well on her way to an exciting thesis body of work, and these pieces are just one example of her unique approach to designing furniture objects that are well-conceived and designed, and function on several levels.

—*Alphonse Mattia, critic*

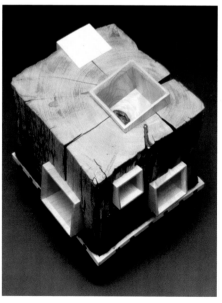

Nest (2004)
David Adams
Rochester (NY) Institute of Technology School for American Craft
Maple, reclaimed barn timber, wool, steel nails
7.625 in. x 8.75 in. x 10.5 in.

Nest evolved as one of a series of pieces developed in graduate study during Dave's wife's pregnancy with their baby son. In Dave's words, "I created several container objects in this series as studies in form, composition, and texture, but as I look back I realize how profoundly the comforting and nesting instincts were manifest in their making. These enigmatic pieces are highly personal, intimate, and textural—all properties that entice us to comfortably explore and handle these objects. Though its origins derive from a conceptual approach to containment, *Nest* may better serve as a display piece than as a storage container." This piece embodies all of the best qualities that we aspire to in our program: strong conceptual depth, adventurous design within a functional context, and outstanding and appropriate craftsmanship.

—*Rich Tannen and Andy Buck, instructors*

Bench (2005)
Michael Albanese
Rochester (NY) Institute of Technology School for American Crafts
Ash, broom corn plant
48 in. x 13 in. x 16 in.

This bench is one of several pieces developed during an MFA thesis investigation incorporating a complementary balance of raw natural materials and those materials and techniques commonly associated with more refined furniture. This piece represents an innovative use of the broom corn plant, commonly used in the construction of brooms. Michael has achieved a seamless integration of the aesthetic and utilitarian roles this material plays in his composition. The straightforward construction, the rhythmic repetition, the texture, and the subtle swirling colors of the broom corn all provide a wonderful complement to the polished ash and the simple, austere geometry of the framework. At the same time, the broom corn creates a very comfortable and inviting surface for seating. The material retains its essential character and is simultaneously transformed into something new.

—*Rich Tannen and Andy Buck, instructors*

Untitled (stool) (2005)
Akiko Yokoyama, Center for Furniture Craftsmanship, ME
Birch veneer
16 in. x 16 in. x 13 in.
Photo: Jim Dugan

This project introduced students to veneering and steam and laminate bending techniques. The brief was to design and build a piece of furniture that incorporates curves and is non-rectilinear, working either in solid wood or veneer, within a five-week period.

Akiko uses model-making intensively as a design tool. Much investigation of folded paper forms inspired by modern packaging resulted in a functional piece that could only be achieved through dogged technical experimentation. The penetration and rhythmic interlocking of the identical segments has resulted in a lightweight object that is both deceptively strong and visually compelling.

—*David Uphill-Brown, instructor*

Dining Table (2005)
Tanya Aquiniga
Rhode Island School of Design
Steel, glass
29 in. x 38 in.

Tanya grew up commuting daily between Tijuana, Mexico, her home, and San Diego, California, where she attended school. She was always thinking about the other side of things, a context she called "the half unseen." The American side represented the land of her education and opportunity, while the Mexican side represented the warmth of family and the vibrant colors, textures, smells, and festivities of her home. This table, constructed of powder-coated welded and laser-cut steel, with glass accessories, explores this notion in a metaphorical manner. In a social setting, what is the "half unseen?" What rests above the table in full view, and what is hidden, secreted away? Aside from creating a beautiful piece that plays with issues of viewing some of what is usually hidden below the table, the piece brings in light in a dramatic way. Shadows and transparencies further the questions of what is real and what is imagined. Though completely utilitarian, the piece has a more poetic side, expressing the intersection of seen and unseen, or of seeing in an unfamiliar way.

—*Rosanne Somerson, professor/critic*

This is part of Hayami's final MFA exhibition work. It is not in response to a specific assignment, but part of a new body of work that combines chair and table forms. Hayami is exploring issues of scale, function, social interaction, and repetition. This first piece in the series is slightly oversized. The sitters have to climb up to get onto the seat. The idea is that the whole piece can serve as a location for a flexible social exchange with users moving around the piece and relating to other individuals, the larger group, or turning their back on the group and facing outward. This piece is typical of Hayami's work in that it uses a traditional Japanese aesthetic combined with a modern take on functional potential.

—*Tom Loeser, instructor*

Kozo (table) (2005)
Hayami Arakawa
University of Wisconsin, Madison
White oak
36 in. x 60 in. x 60 in.
Photo: Hayami Arakawa

NoBody's Chair (2005)
Anthony McCarty
Purchase College, SUNY, School of Art & Design
Poplar, mahogany, paint
39 in. x 30 in. x 42 in.

This exploratory interpretation of the classic Adirondack chair was a collaborative response to a call for entries from Indiana University of Pennsylvania titled: *The Adirondack Chair: Transformation/Reinvention.*

Set up in a tutorial format, this studio class examined the evolution of this unique furniture icon, its stylistic and technical development as well as its cultural underpinnings. Students were challenged to design and construct a contemporary version.

Each student pursued an individual design concept and worked on the collaborative piece. This collaboration might be likened to the revival of the VW beetle—the students determined that they would adhere closely to the original design and materials but incorporate changes that satisfied their design and artistic perspectives, thereby creating a contemporary chair addressing both respect for the primary characteristics of the original design, and a fresh look.

The final product remained true to the directness and simplicity of the original overlap construction, though it did involve some glue-up. By eliminating one arm, it provided for a wider range of sitting options and the opportunity to create a visual dynamic. This chair clearly reminds one of its predecessor yet reflects the contradictions and uncertainties of our cultural environment.

—*Carol Bankerd, Dennis FitzGerald, instructors*

left: Examining Table (2005)
Kate Hudnall, Virginia Commonwealth University
Wood, brass, copper, glass lenses
Photo: Taylor Dagney

Kate Hudnall's work moves into the area of ideas, narrative, and storytelling. She is not a furniture designer with the utilitarian product as her overriding concern. However, Kate isn't eschewing furniture in favor of conceptual sculpture, rather she focuses on the potential meanings and forces a new form of furniture object.

In Kate's thesis, she transformed a small gallery room into a fantastical tinker's workshop. This tinker is an odd sort, obsessive as they always are, needing equally obsessive contraptions and tools such as this observation platform used to analyze what? Or a chess table on swiveling wheels so as to play chess solely with himself.

The craft and woodworking is very purposeful, never relying on the usual postmodern studio furniture "motifs" in forms or finishes. Yet the pieces have an incredible richness, displaying a purposeful history of markings, adaptations, schedules, and measures that this tinker left in the process of making them. The surfaces of objects themselves become a diary of the making and the history of use of the object. In this way, I think they reward the viewer or collector with a new and unique richness of object and furniture form.

—*William Hammersley, instructor*

right: Twist (table) (2005)
Brandon Sherer, Savannah (GA) College of Art & Design
Huesito, Rosita
20 in. x 20 in. x 20 in.
Photo: Wayne Moore

This table is a fine example of an intermediate furniture design project. It fulfills the design brief fully, yet remains simple and uncluttered. The overall craftsmanship is excellent and the choice of woods demonstrates a willingness to explore unusual materials. Formally, the table defines a cube. It is the more subtle details that bring elegance to the work. Rosita miter splines function both structurally and as understated ornament to draw the viewer's eye along the curved bent-laminated Huesito elements to the joint, which punctuates and defines the lower corner of the cube. The sensitive tapering of the horizontal floor support terminates in a delicate tip. The shaping of the dark Rosita underside of the top exhibits an attention to the details and an effort to find not just an adequate resolution of form, but rather, an exceptional one.

—*John Pierson, professor*

Furniture as Prop in the Social Theater of Life

Contemporary sculptors mine furniture for metaphor and raw material

by Jean Blackburn

Coming downstairs, familiar morning smells of coffee and toast flood your consciousness even before your enter the kitchen. You sit in your chair at the kitchen table. Chances are it's a wooden chair or something crumbs can be wiped off of easily, but let's imagine a range of scenarios. It's a well-loved Windsor chair, implying belief in tradition and perhaps harking back to a simpler and more honest time. Maybe the chair is at the head of the table, seat of parental power, surveying the room. No, that would probably be more appropriate at the formal dining room table. Is it a modular, stackable, washable, molded designer piece ordered from a catalogue, proclaiming your efficiency, cleanliness, and hipness, or is it the inherited seat of a departed family member, or the exotic hand-carved piece you had shipped back from your voyage to Madagascar? Or perhaps you are at a café and your chair has been designed to allow you to sit comfortably for about 20 minutes. Does it squat like a frog or sit

above: Table and Chair (Clear) (1994)
Rachel Whiteread
Photo courtesy the artist and Gagosian Gallery, New York and London

Using colored resins, she cast the spaces beneath an ordinary square table with a single chair alongside.

primly with a straight back? Like it or not, before you've had your first sip of coffee, your chair announces a great deal of culturally coded information.

Highly social creatures that we are, we cannot help but read human characteristics into everything around us. The Victorians demonstrated this when they covered shapely furniture legs. In 1938 Kurt Seligmann's *Ultrameuble* used disembodied mannequin legs wearing high white stockings for the legs of his erotically charged table. Tables and chairs could easily have three legs but most commonly have four, for stability certainly but also mimicking our own limbs. Furniture's bisymmetrical structure echoes our bodies. Chairs have arms, legs, backs, and seats (why not laps?). Anthropomorphized, furniture becomes more familiar. Not merely sticks of shaped wood, it reflects us. It feels right.

Certainly it is easy to see maternal qualities represented by some furniture. In *The Poetics of Space,* Gaston Bachelard writes:

> It [the house] maintains him through the storms of the heavens and through those of life. It is body and soul. It is the human being's first world. . . . Life begins well, it begins enclosed, protected, all warm in the bosom of the house.[1]

Like the mother's body, chairs, sofas, and beds cradle and provide respite for their occupants. Wrapped in blankets, pillows, or cushions, furniture envelopes us. Providing refuge is one of the most pleasurable and essential functions of the home and its objects. Frank Lloyd Wright used this as a guiding principle in many of his designs. Perhaps it also explains the popularity of Eero Saarinen's *Womb Chair,* designed in 1948, but back in production today. In recent years, trend trackers and cultural theorists have noted the American desire to cocoon. Everything from overstuffed chairs, SUVs, iPods, computer games, internet shopping, and gated communities reflect this need for insulation and refuge.

How furniture is used and understood changes as economic and social norms evolve. Complex associations with gender and role-playing influence how we perceive the contents of the room. Watch any family sitcom and it will reveal what defines the bastions of male control: typically the garage, the yard, the basement, the recliner, the remote control, the bar, and the grill. Located in the margins of domestic space, this fragmented male fiefdom is symptomatic of women's control of

Editor's note—*Jean Blackburn is a sculptor working near Providence, RI, and professor of art at the Rhode Island School of Design, where she mostly teaches drawing and design. She has exhibited her work widely.*

When Blackburn first offered to write on furniture as material and metaphor in contemporary sculpture, I was thrilled as this has long been an interest of mine and a topic that sheds light on contemporary studio furniture— which, except perhaps for vestigial functionality, may have more in common with sculpture than with anything you could buy at IKEA. Once you accept the idea that provoking thought while filling space is itself a legitimate function, you can have a tough time distinguishing work in these two adjacent fields.

Manuscript in hand, I blithely and enthusiastically began contacting art galleries to request images. Imagine my surprise when I began running into stone walls. The art-world galleries and institutions represented here were extremely generous and helpful. But others, not represented here, recoiled in horror from the very idea that sculpture could be of interest to furniture makers, and that high art could coexist alongside mere furniture.

I tried to explain that this was not the furniture of the department store nor of the 18th century, that the contemporary term "studio furniture" embraced a wide range of objects and artistic intentions, and that Furniture Studio is a serious professional journal. When I could speak with a gallery director I sometimes got a knowing chuckle in reply, though the usual response was silence. I couldn't persuade them to take another look.

Naturally we did a series of end runs around these folks, finding other repositories for the photos we needed.

But along the way I had to marvel at the narrow view those stone walls represented. For not only can furniture makers learn much from contemporary sculptors, but those artists might possibly find something of interest in contemporary furniture. Here's to breaking down the walls and letting in the light.

—*John Kelsey*

As much as the physical furniture itself, these artists are working with its cultural baggage to shape what the sculpture speaks about.

home. Contrast that with pre-industrial times when the successful 18th-century businessman might have used a beautiful mahogany secretary in his home to organize his papers, conduct transactions, and proclaim his economic power. Propriety prescribed appropriate furniture and room layouts for the conducting of business and created a strong masculine presence inside the home—indeed, until Victorian times, it was the man who bought the furniture and furnished the house.

But as cities grew and transportation allowed people to live in the suburbs, business migrated out of the home into urban centers. The mahogany secretary was replaced by the CEO's power desk and, more recently, by the power laptop. Men sought refuge at home from the demands of their jobs, even as they ceded more control of the domestic space to women. The most masculine of men might sleep in a "master bedroom" decorated with feminine ruffles and chintz pillows. This proclaims that the bed is the woman's domain— she invites the man into her bed.

The opposite extreme might be the bachelor pad's king-sized fur-covered bed. The stuff of Hefner mythology, Hollywood, and sports stars, its circular shape dominates the entire room and announces its central importance. It suggests a potential for sexual acrobatics. Here the woman is visiting prey. These subtle messages shape the roles we play and define what is allowed. Furniture plays an essential role as props in the social theatre of our lives.

If the proliferation of home-furnishing stores, mail-order catalogues, decorating and design magazines and TV shows, antique stores, on-line emporiums, and do-it-yourself home building megastores is any indication, public interest in choosing and nuancing what surrounds us at home is at an all-time high. We have so many choices. Through our choices we project our personalities, our social status, and our beliefs.

Many contemporary sculptors have recognized the richly layered language of furniture and the deep resonance of the domestic. For this article, I've selected a few who work extensively with furniture in ways widely recognized as particularly provocative. With Post-Modernism's interest in examining and deconstructing basic cultural assumptions about family, gender roles, and society, the home is a gold mine. It lets us get in at the basement level to see the timbers and foundation on which our cosmos is built. The home shapes what we believe and how we act in the world. Bachelard writes, "For our house is our corner of the world. As has often been said, it is our first

Ultrameuble (1938)
Kurt Seligman
Photo courtesy Orange County
Citizens Foundation, Sugar Loaf, NY

Social creatures that we are, we cannot help but read human characteristics into everything around us.

universe, a real cosmos in every sense of the word."[2] Furniture is an integral and intimate part of that cosmos. While children grow up, furniture helps define important boundaries and embodies the family's values. Posing simple questions will illuminate this. For example, is the dining room table only used for company or Sunday dinner? Do guests ever see an unmade bed? Who decides which sofa to buy and who pays for it? How are gender roles modeled by parents and how is gender associated with objects? Which objects announce our economic or social status? Our understanding of our first home is the point from which all else unfolds. It is the place for sculptors who wish to get at the root of things.

Rachel Whiteread
Casting the voids beneath the chairs

The best work often uses deceptively simple methods to arrive at complex and challenging concepts. Rachel Whiteread's work is a good example. A British sculptor, she is renowned for her remarkable casts of entire rooms and pieces of furniture. She is probably best known for *House* (1993). She covered all the interior walls, windows, doors, and hearths of a London townhouse with plaster, to create a casting that recorded its negative space and surfaces. In effect, she solidified the space inside the house. Later the building was torn down, leaving her casts in place, which she reassembled into a solid block. By transforming space to solid, *House* exposed its vulnerable domestic interior, and entombed its memory.

Whiteread fixated on mold-making and casting early on. As a student at the Slade School of Art she began by molding parts of her own body, such as arm or leg joints, and using these casts to create parallels with pieces of furniture. Next she

House (1993)
Rachel Whiteread
Photos courtesy the artist and Gagosian Gallery, New York and London

Close examination of each casting reveals its individual personality and traces of its history.

moved to molding and casting furniture itself. Always fascinated by hidden spaces, in *Untitled (One Hundred Spaces)*, she cast the voids underneath chairs in translucent resins. She exhibited the resulting geometric forms in a grid that revealed her early Minimalist influence. But closer examination of each casting revealed its individual personality and even traces of its history. A clear homage to Bruce Nauman's *A Cast of the Space under My Chair* (1965–66), the installation echoed an assemblage of absent people. In *Table and Chair (Clear)* (1994), one of a series, she cast the spaces beneath an ordinary square table with a single chair alongside (p. 79). In another piece she cast the inside of a wardrobe similar to one in which she hid as a child. These hidden spaces beneath and inside furniture are places we find and inhabit as children, playing games, hiding, crying. They suggest secrets. We sense vulnerability, discomfort, intimacy, and even fear.

Whiteread's strategy of representing space as a mold or a cast arises from her interest in the body. While casting *House* she came to know its inhabitants well. She comments:

> The house was full of fitted cupboards, cocktail bars and a tremendous variety of wallpapers and floor finishes. I was fascinated by their personal environment and documented it all before I destroyed it. It was like exploring the inside of a body, removing its vital organs. . . . It was as if we were embalming the body.[3]

A bit morbid perhaps, but if the house and its contents can be seen to echo the body, then Whiteread's work addresses the frailty of the body. She strips away the shell. By creating a mold of the physical she records life's tracings. Walls

are cracked, mouldings scratched, rooms are redecorated or reconfigured, buildings are torn down. Whiteread records fleeting configurations. Plaster fills space. Objects become space. Presence and absence, life and death, dwell next to each other, constantly shifting.

Doris Salcedo
Subtle tension in the skin of the surface

The Colombian artist Doris Salcedo is another who uses furniture to respond powerfully to issues of presence, absence, and the body. Compelled to address the horrific violence and civil war that have wracked her country, Salcedo works directly with victims and allows their stories to shape her pieces in what is essentially, for her, an act of mourning. Many of her pieces memorialize the female *desparecidos* or "disappeared." Usually she works with existing local furniture. Worn and marked by use, the surfaces are already rich with association. *La Casa Viuda II* (the Widow's House) (1993–94), collides a door with a drawer-less bureau. The bureau barricades the door. Together they form the simple shape of a chair, suggesting both presence

La Casa Viuda II (the Widow's House) (1993–94), overall and detail
Doris Salcedo
Photos courtesy the artist and Art Gallery of Ontario, gift from the Volunteer Committee Fund, 1997

Compelled to address the horrific violence and civil war that have wracked her country, Colombia, Salcedo works directly with victims and allows their stories to shape her pieces in an act of mourning.

and absence. Into the deep varnished surface of the top of the bureau, Salcedo has embedded a sharp splinter of bone and several small white buttons. Along the side, tucked subtly between a panel and a frame of the bureau, is a half-open zipper. The critic Nancy Princenthal writes:

> Though small and covert, these details are clearly visible. But to describe them in terms that lead to explicit associations with the human body is slightly misleading: such links, though real, are so subtle as to seem fugitive, even imaginary. Moreover, the most telling details seem to enter consciousness at least in part through touch (even when, as is generally the case, touching is prohibited), an uncanny effect. . . evocations of the human through garments, with their closeness and likeness to skin—indeed, references to bodies as direct as the use of bones themselves—are made to seem like inert, foreign elements in the living bodies of wooden furniture. The lace, the buttons and the bone mark sites where the skin of chairs and chest of drawers is rubbed raw; in effect these elements become, despite their obvious frailty, the instruments by which those wounds are inflicted.[4]

Salcedo was trained as a painter. Her ability to create subtle sensation comes from sensitivity to the skin of the surface. At times her working of the surface is immensely laborious. In *The Orphan's Tunic,* two wooden tables have been jammed together and the legs where they overlap have been broken off. The piece was inspired by a 6-year-old girl, who after witnessing her mother's murder, refused to stop wearing the silk tunic her mother had made for her. Frayed, ghostly white silk intimately binds itself to the surface of one table. Just where the silk frays and becomes the wood surface, miraculously, Salcedo creates a band of thick brown hair by threading it through tiny holes in the wood. The silk and the hair give such delicate tactility and pathos to the simple gesture of the tables that we are drawn in slowly and deeply. Salcedo's careful craftsmanship focuses the stillness and silence of the pieces. We are meant to contemplate events that language cannot easily encompass.

Salcedo sees Colombian society as a mix of feudal and modern industrial elements. Her pieces reflect this uncomfortable hybridization. She uses worn furniture, marked, some handmade and some mass-produced. In many pieces she fills wooden cabinets, dressers, or armoires with cement. In a particularly memorable piece, *Untitled* (1998), a delicately decorated cabinet merges into a doorless dark wood armoire. The space they share inside the armoire is filled with cement, weighty, blocking any movement or function. The cabinet, only half visible, seems to be dissolving into the cement. This collision of individual and industrial materials suggests brutality and loss. We feel intimately the lives lived around these objects. But these lives are broken, stunted, mute and missing. Salcedo reminds us just how deeply domestic tranquility has been betrayed. Her pieces suggest the power of violence to cripple physically, psychologically, and spiritually.

Andrea Zittel
Art products propose a way of life

Andrea Zittel also is keenly interested in how the house and its furniture shelter and define our living activities. Zittel creates "living units" designed and "marketed" by her company A-Z (a play on her own initials). Reductivist in nature,

More than simply postulating a solution for various domestic problems through her "products," Zittel's larger project proposes a way of life.

these units facilitate essential life functions with a Spartan use of space. Pieces such as *A-Z Dishless Dining Table* (1993) and *A-Z Raugh Dishless Dining Table* (1999) echo the efficiency found in Shaker objects, boat interiors, and Modernist design. This sparseness could suggest ecological responsibility. Her formats have included modular mats, cubicles, trailers, and escape pods, as seen in *Cellular Compartment Units* (2001). On numerous occasions, she has lived in her pieces, simultaneously engaging in "test-marketing" and performance art.

Zittel's exhibition brochure for the A-Z Living Unit, shown at the Jack Hanley Gallery in 1993, intones in Utopian market-speak:

> Think of being able to own your own home and being able to bring it along wherever you go.... Think of being able to create a small nucleus designed to perfectly accommodate just your needs... a nucleus that has the ability to remain constant even when surroundings are ever-changing.[6]

By parodying companies that sell products to enhance our lifestyles and our well-being, and by interacting with her pieces, Zittel embraces a complex of issues. More than simply postulating a solution for various domestic problems through her products, her larger project proposes a way

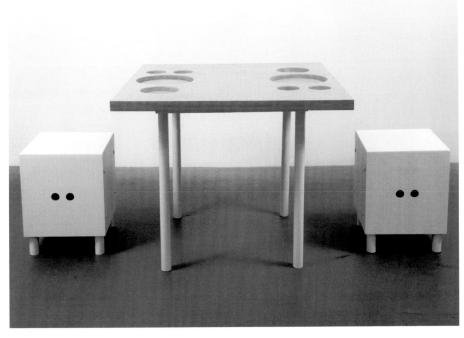

facing page: A-Z Raugh Dishless Dining Table (1999)
Andrea Zittel
wood, metal, paint;
29 in. x 59 in. x 30 in.
Goetz Collection, Munich

left: A-Z Dishless Dining Table (1993)
Andrea Zittel
Wood, steel, paint; table;
29 in. x 36 in. x 36 in.,
stools: 18 in. x 14 in. x 14 in.
Goetz Collection, Munich

Photos courtesy the artist and
Andrea Rosen Gallery, New York

These pieces echo the efficiency found in Shaker objects, boat interiors, and Modernist design and could suggest ecological responsibility.

of life. She is conceiver, creator, marketer, and consumer of her products. This strategy also allows her to be depersonalized, Utopian, the "we" of a company as well as the individual confronting and interpreting the piece. In paring living down to its most elemental functions, Zittel represents a radical, efficient, almost puritanical model for living. It may be seen as controlling and limited, or conversely, as freeing from rampant and superfluous materialism. It echoes social utopias espoused by the Bauhaus and Soviet artists in the early 20th century. But instead of manifestos, Zittel presents a marketing brochure. Ironically, her Utopian creations are distributed through elite capitalistic galleries. Potentially attacking the system they participate in, her pieces can be seen to function as Trojan Horses.[7]

Allan Wexler
Complex structures for simple tasks

Allan Wexler shares Zittel's interest in domestic function and efficiency. But unlike Zittel, his pieces are not Utopian, and instead make more evident the imperfect, the individualistic, the handmade. Take, for instance, his description of *Building for Formal Dining* (1981):

> I first made four chairs spontaneously, imprecisely built so that each chair is unique. I then used the back braces of each chair to define the position for the edges of the table. Because each of the braces occurs at a different location on the chair, the table top is uneven and

Vinyl Milford House (1994), exterior and interior
Allan Wexler
Photo courtesy Ronald Feldman Fine Arts, New York

The house's kitchen, bathroom, bedroom, and dining room cannot all coexist at the same time, so Wexler built extensions onto the walls to house the furniture and equipment for the rooms.

slopes down toward the center. The legs of the chairs fit into grooves in the floor, forcing the occupants to move only in straight paths perpendicular to the table edges. The final architecture of the building depends on those four imprecise chairs.[8]

Of course it is a paradox that accumulated imperfections should ultimately shape a building designed to shelter formal dining furniture. Despite their individuality, the chairs can make only very limited movement. Wexler suggests both the social strictures of formal dining and the limited definitions that architecture itself allows.

In *Vinyl Milford House* (1994), Wexler begins with the form of a vinyl-covered mass-produced steel storage shed. Because the shed is so small, the house's requisite kitchen, bathroom, bedroom, and dining room cannot all coexist at the same time. To accommodate, Wexler builds extensions onto the walls to house the furniture and equipment for the rooms. When a particular room is required, the appropriate furniture is pulled out from the wall. Bulging from the exterior walls, these extensions betray their simple configurations in silhouette.

In both pieces, constrained movements and formalized social behavior transform the building into a ritualized space. It is not surprising that Wexler lists among his influences the Japanese tea ceremony, non-Western music, and ancient religions. By ritualizing the mundane, Wexler highlights the "theater of everyday life."[9] He uses an architectural pedestal to set

the space and the actions apart. Thus they can be contemplated, and the everyday moment elevated.

In other pieces Wexler collides several functional objects to produce an absurd hybrid. As the resulting object struggles for definition, we contemplate the original functional objects with fresh eyes. He writes of *Screen Chair*, a piece he created in 1991:

> *Screen Chair* is simultaneously a porch and a chair. Here I continued my exploration of the relationship of the human body and architecture, and of architecture and furniture. Flat rectangular planes clothe the body and isolate the various parts of the human anatomy, contrasting the angular and the organic. Constructed of insect screening, the chair refers both to the cocoon and to the front porch. It protects the occupant from, while at the same time connecting her to, nature.[10]

Screen Chair (1991)
Allan Wexler
Photo courtesy Ronald Feldman Fine Arts, New York

Like Rube Goldberg's hilarious chain reactions, the pieces get a humorous charge by using complex structures to accomplish simple tasks.

Wexler was trained as an architect. Using a rule of thumb for any good architect, Wexler's form does follow function, but the function is often absurd. Like Rube Goldberg's hilarious chain reactions, the pieces get a humorous charge by using complex structures to accomplish simple tasks.

Wexler has presented many of his ideas as maquettes, in the tradition of the miniature architectural model. When viewing these pieces we imagine them in use. We play in our heads. Childlike, we imagine sliding parts out, opening drawers, sitting at the tiny seats. We have the pleasure of changing size like Alice in Wonderland. This playful imagining, so much part of childhood and running throughout Wexler's work, gives his pieces great resonance. But these are also models— ideas about furniture and architecture pared

down to their most simple configurations. Because emphasis is on the configuration rather than the particular style or material of the furniture, the pieces can't be locked into a particular movement or decade. We can float in time. Again in *The Poetics of Space,* Bachelard describes the importance of that free association through time:

> The house. . . will permit me. . . to recall flashes of daydreams that illuminate the synthesis of immemorial and recollected. In this remote region, memory and imagination remain associated, each one working for their mutual deepening. . . they both constitute a community of memory and image. Thus the house is not experienced from day to day only, on the thread of a narrative, or in the telling

Under the Table (1994)
Robert Therrien
Installation view, Santa Fe Depot, San Diego
Photo: Philipp Scholz Ritterman, courtesy the artist and SITE Santa Fe

We feel protected under the roof of the table. But we are afraid of whoever sits in these chairs.

of our own story. Through dreams, the various dwelling-places in our lives co-penetrate and retain the treasures of former days.[11]

Playful imagining allows us to associate the richness of past experience with the present. Wexler wisely gives us enough to engage our imaginations and experiences, but not so much that we are excluded. His simplified forms are universal and iconic. When these are coupled with simple mundane actions like sitting at the dining room table or on the porch, we feel the universality of our simplest actions, their humor and their humanity.

Robert Therrien
Experiences rooted in childhood memory

If we delight in the dollhouse scale of Wexler's models, we ourselves shrink to toddler size alongside some of Robert Therrien's memorable pieces. In *Under the Table* (1994), Therrien recreates a simple iconic table and chairs at an enormous size. While the furniture is stylistically unremarkable, the scale change snaps us back to the vulnerability we felt as children living in a land of giants. It affects the way we perceive our bodies in space. We feel protected under the roof of the table. But we are afraid of whoever sits in these chairs. It is no longer simply a functional table. We see its underside. The combination of the mundane and the extraordinary forces us to reconsider familiar objects. Our response is tangled in early memories and subjective associations.

In other pieces Therrien creates an enormous stack of dishes or a gigantic keyhole. A long-time member of the Los Angeles art scene, Therrien's elasticity of scale has important precedence in cartoons, trippy '60's graphics, Hollywood, Dada, and Surrealism. The objects he chooses to represent are very familiar. They elicit a fairly standard response. Yet his distortions throw us into a new realm. As in Wexler's work, rationalism shows its limitations. Therrien seems to be searching for something deeper, more rooted in the body's experience and childhood memory.

Template (2002)
Jean Blackburn
Photo courtesy the artist

As the larger chair is consumed, its form becomes more obscure and we must refer to the smaller chair to envision it whole.

Jean Blackburn
Removing material to manipulate it

In my own sculpture, I usually start with a piece of used furniture. Since it is a functional object with a history and revealing surfaces, it provides a lot to respond to. Often a piece of furniture will sit in my studio for months as I assess its qualities. What can it speak about? What are its material or structural limitations? Once this is resolved, I begin removing material from the furniture so it can be manipulated, reconfigured, and built back into the piece. By cutting parts out from the furniture and using the removed materials to build new structures I can suggest that like us, they are in a process of redefinition.

Materials excavated from a large wooden rocking chair are used to create a perfect miniature in *Template* (2002). As the larger chair is consumed, its form becomes more obscure and we must refer to the smaller chair to envision it whole. The two depend on each other. Their definition and dissolution are intertwined. In another piece, an upholstered chair, potentially a comfortable place to relax, is interwoven with parts of dishtowels, bed sheets, and napkins. Alluding to many of the tasks of housekeeping, cleaning, privacy, display, rest, and work, *Serviette* (2002) ultimately presents the viewer with a small decorative hand towel. The viewer takes on the role of a guest. Too small and delicate to actually use, these hand towels have always seemed the height of absurd display. They only come out when guests arrive. Family can't use them. They are meant to suggest hospitality. But no one actually wipes their grubby hands on them.

These pieces are meant to echo domestic relationships and situations. Materials grow into each other and new structures emerge, at the cost of older ones. Some things are nurtured or echoed in delicate structures, while others are plundered for material or left to wither. These processes echo some of the harsh realities and unpleasant truths that crop up even in the most ideal domestic circumstances. If I am successful, my manipulations cause a reassessment of the object and, by extension, some aspect of domestic or contemporary life.

Marcel Duchamp
In debt to the ready-made

As we have seen, almost any domestic object or piece of furniture comes with a lot of baggage. We live with it every day. We know the history behind its most intimate scratches and dents. We might compare a dining room chair with other chairs we have known, or associate it with a specific period in time. Unlike traditional sculptors who create forms from raw materials, most of the sculptors I have discussed begin with existing structures. These existing structures might be the configuration of a London townhouse, as in Whiteread's work, used furniture as in Salcedo's work or my own, or a mass-produced form like Wexler's vinyl shed. Zittel and Therrien play off of common cultural stereotypes and idealized

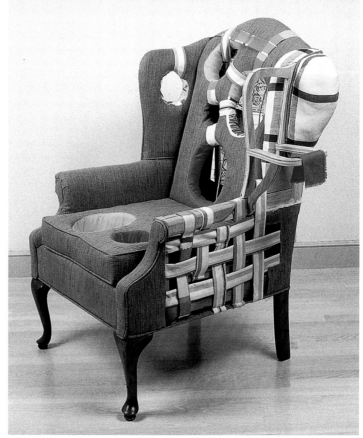

Serviette (2002)
Jean Blackburn
Photo courtesy the artist

These pieces echo domestic relationships and situations. Materials grow into each other and new structures emerge, at the cost of older ones.

forms to suggest Utopian or dysfunctional realities. As much as the physical furniture itself, these artists are working with its cultural baggage to shape what the sculpture speaks about. These existing forms provide a framework of ideas with which the artists can interact.

In 1913 when Marcel Duchamp joined a bicycle wheel upside-down to a stool, and created the concept of a "ready-made," he revolutionized what could be considered art. *Bicycle Wheel* is disarmingly simple, but it forces the viewer to contemplate the relationship between active and static form, between the conceptual and the functional. Once joined, the bicycle wheel cannot roll and the stool cannot be sat on. Functionally they cancel each other out. Besides joining them, Duchamp presents the objects exactly as he found them. Clearly *Bicycle Wheel* isn't about traditional craftsmanship. It is about the juxtaposition of concepts that the objects embody. Duchamp works with ready-mades because the concepts are more pure, less prone to personal

Bicycle Wheel (ready-made) (1913)
Marcel Duchamp
Photo courtesy Philadelphia Museum of Art

Duchamp works with ready-mades because the concepts are more pure, less prone to personal interpretation, than handmade objects. His craft is in honing ideas so they fit as seamlessly as an exquisitely dovetailed joint. These artists all owe some debt to Marcel Duchamp's ready-mades.

interpretation, than handmade objects. His craft is in honing ideas so they fit as seamlessly as an exquisitely dovetailed joint.

The artists I've mentioned all owe some debt to Marcel Duchamp's ready-mades. All have chosen to work with well-established furniture forms. These artists are not trying to design effective pieces of furniture, they are trying to address larger cultural issues embodied in or symbolized by the furniture. The furniture forms function as a kind of raw material. Zittel is the only one who attempts to improve on the objects she creates, but it is always in service to her larger social agenda. In Whiteread's and Salcedo's works, personal objects are used and narratives are suggested. The style or construction of a table might be a matter of curiosity, but it is not the point. The furniture functions to suggest the

lives of people, both present and absent. For these artists, using an Art Deco chair would limit associations to a particular decade or social class. More universal notions such as the chair as a place to sit, as a presence or absence, or as a location in space, could be simply addressed with a more stylistically neutral chair. The idea of the "ready-made" continues to resonate because furniture is so rich in associations. We live with it every day. It surrounds us as we grow up and shape our ideas about the world. It comes to embody our histories, our values, and our hopes for the future.

Notes

1. Gaston Bachelard, *The Poetics of Space.* Translated by Maria Jolas. (Boston: Beacon Press, 1969), p. 7.

2. Ibid., p. 4.

3. Beatriz Colomina, "I Dreamt I Was a Wall," *Rachel Whiteread: Transient Spaces,* (N.Y., N.Y.: Guggenheim Museum Pub., 2002) pp. 77–78. Colomina quoted from: "Rachel Whiteread Interviewed by Andrea Rose," *Rachel Whiteread: British Pavilion, 47th Venice Biennial, exh. cat.* (London: British Arts n All Gallagher, ed Council, 1997), p. 33i.

4. Nancy Princenthal, "Silence Seen," *Doris Salcedo,* (London: Phaidon Press, 2000), p. 60.

5. Op Cit. Bachelard, p. 5.

6. *Andrea Zittel.* Essays by Ingvild Goetz, Rainald Schumacher, and Mimi Zeiger. (Munich: Ingvild Goetz, Rainald Schumacher, 2003), p. 68, quoted from exhibition brochure for the Jack Hanley Gallery, (San Francisco, 31.3–1.5, 1993).

7. *Andrea Zittel.* Essays by Ingvild Goetz, Rainald Schumacher, and Mimi Zeiger. (Munich: Ingvild Goetz, Rainald Schumacher, 2003), p. 76.

8. Gustau Gili Galfetti ed., Quote by the Artist, *Alan Wexler.* (Barcelona, GG Portfolio, 1998), p. 16.

9. Ibid. p. 14

10. Ibid. p. 35.

11. Op Cit. Bachelard, pp. 5–6.

The Tension Between Design and Art

Roy McMakin's A Slat-back Chair, *at San Diego State University, June 2005*

by Don R. Miller

The Furniture Society's presentation of Roy McMakin's *A Slat-back Chair* at the recent San Diego conference represents a significant step in broadening the organization's vision and constituency. Tina Yapelli, director of the University Art Gallery at San Diego State University, and Wendy Maruyama, head of the furniture program there, deserve congratulations for envisioning an exhibition that combines contemporary concerns in design and sculpture with the more craft-based vantage point that the Furniture Society has represented. Response to the show indicated that, as our membership embraces a wider view of the furniture world, thoughtful dialog will be a necessary alternative to factionalism. This

exhibition was such an opportunity. This review is based on several great ongoing conversations I had in San Diego—conversations that directed me through simplistic reactions to a more meaningful experience of McMakin's work.

My initial response to *A Slat-back Chair* was mixed. I recognized Roy McMakin as one of a group of "design artists" who in the past several years have become known for work that, oddly enough, concerns the boundaries between contemporary art and design. As a furniture maker, I consider myself slightly removed from this hybrid practice. Part purist, part Luddite, I thrive on work that exists on the edges of traditional hierarchies, and

facing page: *Untitled* (2001)
Roy McMakin
Photo by Mark Woods

above: *Untitled (Would Dining
Table and Six Simple Chairs)* (2005)
Roy McMakin
Photo by Mark Woods

pondering new ideas is an important aspect of my studio and teaching experiences. I've given some consideration to "design art" and had concluded that while conceptually interesting, it offers little of the exciting experience that I find in the rub between function and art. And yet, I continued to be interested in the tension that is central to the work of these artists.

So how did I initially respond to the exhibition? I was impatient that McMakin's work fashionably referred to the furniture-based works of Donald Judd and Scott Burton, that it appropriated these without clear attribution. The work appeared concise, industrial in character, its surfaces a bit too perfect. Its reduction of the furniture idiom felt awkward, unbalanced but predictable. The scale of these furniture pieces, here presented

Don Miller makes furniture in Cranston, RI, and is adjunct faculty at Rhode Island School of Design. A catalog entitled A Slat-back Chair *accompanied the exhibition (ISBN 0-937097-02-0) and is available from the University Art Gallery, San Diego State University.*

as autonomous works of sculpture, seemed timid and rather arbitrary. The accompanying drawings distracted from the work, rather than focusing it. But almost immediately I found myself questioning these initial responses and, by watching and asking, queried other responses. Evidently, this work is provocative. What lies beneath its surface?

Viewed as a continuum rather than a spread of individual objects, *A Slat-back Chair* effectively displaces the viewer's experience of space. McMakin makes us immediately aware of the human-scale space within which we navigate and that we project upon furniture objects. He asks us to respond not to the unique character of these objects but to their familiar and essentially mundane qualities. It is in this intimate, everyday territory that we engage with the work, completing it with our own participation as viewers/users. In experiencing it, we experience ourselves.

As makers, we sometimes dismiss work that asks us to consider more than its formal qualities or technical character. We tend to be too literal, too close. Furniture, on one hand, does convey meaning to us via its purely didactic character: it can express a clear historical style, construction technique, use of material, or representational narrative. However, furniture's character as a phenomenon, a means to experience, underlies this rational notion. Furniture's phenomenological character is inextricably linked to our navigation of the physical universe, in gravity and in space. From it springs our first and most basic sensibilities of what is real, and our metaphors for what is less so. As primary influences on the development of our conscious and subconscious beings, everyday objects come to be the real and symbolic measures of one's place in the world, the meeting of memory and moment.

Roy McMakin's work in *A Slat-back Chair* peels through the layers of meaning we perceive in and project onto furniture objects. His objects appear too familiar, too generic, to spark strong responses.

Untitled (Would Dining Table and Six Simple Chairs) (2005) detail
Roy McMakin
Photo by Mark Woods

Nightstand (1999)
Roy McMakin
Photo by Mark Woods

But this formally reductive approach is what allows tensions to enter the work. This energy lies as much in the context McMakin has created for the work, and in the participation of the viewer/user, as in its objective presence as a group of simple chairs. This strategy reflects an ongoing concern with the ideals of Modernism, a desire to interrogate and transform those values rather than react against them. Throughout the 20th century, design innovation led the way in challenging the academic separation of art from everyday experience. Avant-gardes pulled art and design into the streets in rejection of the academy's grip on culture. These ideals were ultimately addressed by Minimalist sculptors whose large-scale, industrially fabricated works brought the viewer into the space of the work to determine his own point of view, her own experience. These works were as much the progeny of design and architecture as of sculpture. In the 70s and 80s artists such as Donald Judd, Scott Burton, and Richard Artschwager found the history of furniture design, particularly that of the early 20th century, a source of inspiration—Wright, Stickley, Rietveld, and Bauhaus. Their choice to make sculptures based in furniture form, scale, and materials expressed a desire to democratize the culture of art, continuing a revolution begun at the turn of the century to render the art object ubiquitous, available in everyday experience and contingent upon the viewer's participation and understanding.

The baking of preconceived notions: Another take on Roy McMakin

The McMakin gallery at San Diego State University was a passable walk from the Furniture Society conference center, and given the buzz, the hike gave conference-goers time to form and bake their preconceived responses. It was a very provocative exhibition, and any discussion, pre-, during- or post-conference was well worth the effort. In fact, McMakin bashing and praising by furniture devotees is ongoing in e-mails and chat rooms.

You can read furniture maker Don Miller's reaction to the exhibit in the accompanying review. My own first reaction to the exhibition was that one had entered a stark, edgy (NY) downtown gallery—not surprising given McMakin's current Chelsea representatives—or an equally stark and edgy loft apartment just before the guests arrive for the party. White-on-white around and above; polished wood floor; cool and diffuse gallery lighting. The installation was primarily of chairs that on first impression were all, if not the same, then decidedly very similar. They were lined up in small to large groups along the walls, giving the space a curiously 17th century twist.

McMakin has taken this all-too familiar Reform School Revival chair and made it new again. He set out to explore a banal furniture form with the intent of exposing its innate design quality and giving it new and better life. But where Marcel Duchamp's ready-made urinal fountain did this with a smack to the side of the intellectual head, and Pop artists overwhelmed us with outrageous color, McMakin has chosen to make his influence as subtle and nuanced as possible. He relies on Minimalist tweaking, with each chair being pushed in a slightly different direction. As Don Miller notes, the understatement is tremendously effective and induces the viewer to dwell on each piece, to discover and savor each juicy detail. Most of chairs were not varnished, but subtly and exquisitely painted in various shades of white, and most viewers were startled to discover that it was all brush-applied, no doubt rubbed out, but meticulously beautiful nonetheless.

The chairs aside, a favorite piece for viewing and discussing was a matte-varnished, dark oak dining table accompanied by six of what McMakin calls "simple chairs." Upon close inspection, one became aware of long, rectangular filler pieces—dutchmen—inlaid over rusty nail holes, knots and other visual defects, allowing for visual play on the surface. This is not a new idea, but since it is a signature technique it is worth noting that examination of later tables, some in walnut and other, more carefully selected woods, reveals an evolution and refinement of the vocabulary well beyond arbitrary table-top decoration in recycled material. In McMakin's hands it is a playful, deliberate maneuver to catch the eye just as it was wondering about joint interfaces that have been artificially rotated or moved from one orientation to another by skillful application of inlay. It is a wonderful effect.

Because of the neo-banality of the furniture, many viewers needed a little nudge-nudge, wink-wink in order to take notice and begin to make these discoveries. The furniture benefits from a sympathetic interior, and even better, the deliberate context of a gallery installation like the SDSU gallery, or better yet a trendy loft like the one in New York City where I saw a newer version of the table. The wood was walnut, and the two-piece top included some subtle wisps of sapwood book-matched along the glue line. The oily finish of the first table had shifted to a soft sheen, and the rectangular inlays were perfectly executed and carefully placed. The table was in a dining area visible from the living area but two steps down, affording a side-on view that revealed such intricate delicacies as a slight dado between the top and the apron, and a weightlessness-inducing float due to small spacers under the heavy square legs.

McMakin has produced some silly pieces, such as *Nightstand* (facing page) or a chest of drawers laid on its back with its glass "top" sitting on the drawer faces, but when he gets serious, he delivers cutting-edge freshness and excitement. The buzz is for real.

—*Michael Podmaniczky,*
  chair, Furniture Studio Editorial Advisory Board

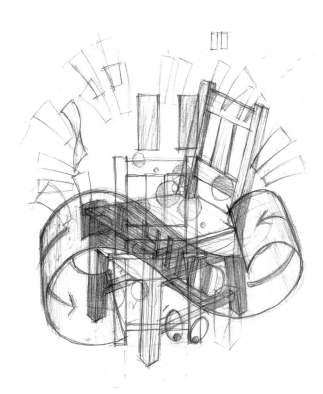

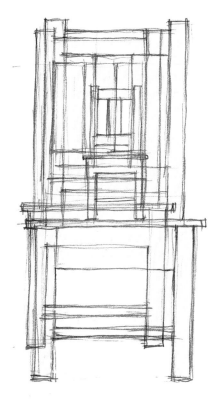

top: Untitled (2005)
Drawing by Roy McMakin

bottom: Untitled (2005)
Drawing by Roy McMakin

top: Untitled (2005)
Drawing by Roy McMakin

bottom: Untitled (2005)
Drawing by Roy McMakin

McMakin, along with such artists as Andrea Zittel (page 84), Clay Ketter, Jorge Pardo, and Joe Scanlan, has carried on this investigation of the rub between everyday objects, our personal lives, and our culture. Contemporary "design artists" create conceptual frameworks for their work that are self-consciously distinct from those of their Modernist predecessors and are integral with, rather than supplemental to, their work. Zittel, for example established AZ Industries as her first artwork, a fictitious corporate backdrop against which to present her one-off "products." At heart these artists' ideas respond to, react against, and reinterpret the questions that Modernism posed regarding the autonomy of the artwork, the immutability of artistic intent, and the distinctions between high and low culture. Often as theoretically rigorous as it is humorously ironic, this loose confederation of artists values popular culture over high culture, the marketplace over the museum, relativity over absolutism, experience over ideology. The fetish objects of high Modernism, say an Eames LCW chair or a Noguchi coffee table, are

Simple Chair (1995)
Roy McMakin
Photo by Mark Woods

Plain Chair, 1988 (built 1998)
Roy McMakin
Photo by Mark Woods

simultaneously revered as icons and debunked as the remnants of a self-contradicting ideology, as both art and as anthropological artifact. "Design art" reflects the values of today's post-industrial global consumer culture back on itself, hoping for a glint of recognition in the paradox revealed by its nostalgia for the simpler, more stable cultural identity of the 1950s. This self-critique suggests we are what we buy, and regards commodities as inseparable from the context of their manufacture, advertising, and purchase. Design artists appear to revel in this reality, seizing it as an opportunity to make artworks from a new cultural perspective. As artist Joe Scanlan writes, "…design art hopes to democratize [cultural] authority by providing mood lighting and comfortable chairs. Institutional critique is based on argumentation; design art on salesmanship."

Design art raises some interesting questions from within its own back yard. Scanlan sums up a basic concern when he writes, "…invoking design and function as a foil for making art betrays a troubling lack of nerve." He goes on to criticize those artists "…whose need for art to appear useful—without

Untitled (Chair with Hole in Wall) (2005) computer rendering
Roy McMakin
Rendering by Scott Graczyk

the risk of being so—strikes us as timid and sad." At its most effective, "design art" inspires the viewer to think carefully about art, design, and craft, and about their constantly shifting relationships to consumer culture. It recognizes the cultural eloquence of functional objects and is intent on employing that quality in ever more subtle ways by emphasizing shifting contexts and meanings. On the down side, some design art flattens the milieu of everyday objects into abstractions, divorced from provenance and use—aesthetic commodities ready for appropriation and consumption. Scanlan describes an attitude that views art objects first of all as commodities. Function becomes a transient fashion, an entertainment, rather than a core experience. But perhaps that's exactly the point.

McMakin's work fits uneasily into this genre. His practice exhibits a synthesis of art making, collaboration and entrepreneurship that has identified design/art fusions since the early 20th century. McMakin self-consciously refers to himself as a "concept generator" rather than claiming any of the many hats he wears—that of artist, designer, woodworker, painter, illustrator, architect, businessman. But in this sense he resembles a Renaissance polyglot more than a Postmodern impresario. The breadth of McMakin's furniture-related experience enhances the richness of his work's context. While his most basic visual vocabulary refers to an aesthetic of industrial production, the work denies such easy categorization. There are plenty of slippages in what the context of production and distribution actually is, but these lend a subtle solidity to the work rather than any backhanded irony. Its minimal character becomes a pallet for a broader viewer experience. This potential fills out the work as one looks closer and gleans more about its understated presence and provenance. Its formal simplicity and meticulously executed, almost

*above, left: Untitled
(Painting Chair)* (2003)
Roy McMakin
Photo by Mark Woods

*above, right: Untitled
(Sculpture Chair)* (2005)
Roy McMakin
Photo by Mark Woods

left: Untitled Chair Set (2005)
computer rendering
Roy McMakin
Rendering by Scott Graczyk

industrial workmanship leave little evidence of the subjective hand of the maker. As such the work becomes an abstraction of the handmade. When subjective marks are evident, they read even more strongly (and strangely!) by being framed as such by the surrounding minimal context. This highly self-conscious, conceptual evidence of craft parallels a similar and more subtle historicism that reveals itself to the viewer via a deep (yet strange!) familiarity of form. This experience and resulting conceptual framework emerges through the senses rather than through didactic catalog entries or placards on the gallery wall.

McMakin describes his collaboration with the furniture makers at Bigleaf Manufacturing as "…an almost Utopian quest to make perfect things in an imperfect world." His choices to focus on the quality and provenance of materials, and his one-off/batch approach to production, are noteworthy. The work's surprising handmade character relates more to the values of contemporary studio furniture than to those of contemporary design/art. Without employing the formal vocabulary of a more craft-based ideology, he is able to reflect that value system in forms that are unfamiliar.

Two-Part Chairs, Obtuse Angle (A Pair) (1983–1984)
Scott Burton
granite, 33 x 24 x 33 in. each
Collection Walker Art Center, Minneapolis
Gift of the Butler Family Fund, 1984

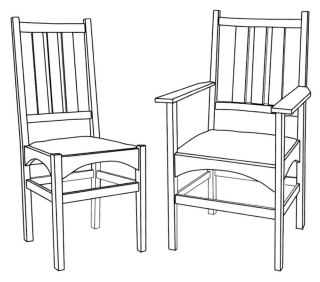

No. 353 Side Chair, Gustav Stickley

He's not a maker, but he acknowledges and employs the eloquence of the handmade object over the mass-produced. McMakin benefits from working at the distance of a designer, but he recognizes the empathetic power of the handmade—the dynamic that sparks between making and using. He channels this empathy from a distance that allows the work both its handmade nature and a more conceptual character at the same time. It is this quality of an object held in tension that also holds my interest.

David Pye, in *The Nature and Art of Workmanship*, emphasizes the importance of definition and distinction when discussing the relationship between design and workmanship. Pye differentiates, "Design is what, for practical purposes, can be conveyed in words and drawing: workmanship is what, for practical purposes, can not." For practical purposes. He notes that the qualities of "good" workmanship are often misattributed to "good" design. Similarly, he suggests that there is no such thing as inherently "good material" but rather material that has been made good by the investment of workmanship. Quality, or rather a diverse range of qualities, is the outcome of a symbiosis between appropriate design and appropriate workmanship.

above: *Untitled Chairs* (1987)
Donald Judd
multiple colors of Finland Color Plywood
Photo: Judd Furniture ©Judd Foundation 2006

right: *Chair* (1966)
Richard Artschwager
Formica on wood, 59 x 16 x 30 inches
©2006 Richard Artschwager/Artists Rights Society
Photo: Gagosian Gallery, New York

Pye limits himself to a practical treatment of these concerns to describe a critical language with which to discuss workmanship and its contemporary context. But Pye, in a more abstract sense, is also describing the balance of distance and empathy that is essential to any creative act or aesthetic experience.

The practical symbiotic relationship that Pye describes is of great importance to the success of McMakin's work. His collaboration with Bigleaf yields more than the sum of its parts. On one hand, the relationship lends its products a specific character of quality, through the sensitive use of renewable materials, one-off manufacture, and small-scale distribution. The McMakin/Bigleaf partnership has clearly benefited from the practical relationship that Pye discusses. But the dialectic that exists between design and making benefits this work on a deeper level. It focuses the potential of well-designed, well-made objects to express ideas and experiences, concepts and phenomena, the quantifiable and the inexpressible. McMakin's work balances the distance from which design conceptualizes against the empathy that quality workmanship elicits. This balance of distance with empathy is at the core an individual's aesthetic

experience, and it is the lens through which I found myself experiencing much of this work.

The exhibition is accompanied by dozens of drawings that depict not only the formal, linear nature of design process, but drawing as repetition, as meditation. McMakin's drawings become responses and addenda to the pieces, as well as documents of their development. They serve a range of purposes from practical to humorous, lending the work a broadly ironic character. They are concepts, designs, half of Pye's equation for a well-met object.

Le Corbusier Chair (1990)
Jorge Pardo
Welded copper pipes
26 x 30 x 33.25 in.

As for the work, much of the exhibition consists of variations on a single generic slat-backed chair reminiscent of the simple turn-of-the-century Stickley designs found in every school principal's anteroom. A reductive approach to structure, simplicity and consistency of proportions and use of materials, and straightforward choices of traditional construction methods all refer to this iconic form. As an object of material culture, the slat-backed chair speaks in simple detail about the cultural upheaval that accompanied the passage of the 19th century: industrialization, Utopianism, commodification, and the aesthetic of the machine.

The exhibition begins with a set of simple formal variations. The basic chair is sequentially altered via changes in proportion, color, texture, and mass/volume—each with a title, name, and identity. Variations of simple structural details become a formal language, a means of documenting the viewer's evolving experience. The setting is at once sensually charged and mundane, an uneasy hybrid of art and life. McMakin presents this essential paradox in a variety of guises throughout the exhibition. Immediately one is frustrated by the physical inaccessibility of the work. These

are chairs after all—one wants to touch and sit. But the presentation emphasizes the hands-off nature of the gallery setting, turning apparently functional objects into "useless" art objects. By way of introduction, our presumptions, assumptions regarding what we see, how we look, and how we use, are being challenged. By focusing the viewer's attention, these chairs also displace it.

A second group of slat-backed chairs eliminates most formal variation. These untitled pieces serve instead as generic vehicles for perceptual improvisations in the surrounding space, the space we navigate. By emphasizing this negative space around each neutral grey/white form, the voids between back slats, stretchers, and rails are reduced to primary delineations of the surrounding space— a Constructivist abstraction. Mirrors fill some of the spaces between chair elements, further displacing the viewer's gaze. As the center of one's experience shifts from the object to the space around it, the familiarity of perception and consciousness becomes mutable, relative. The work subtly leaves the domain of furniture, of everyday events, and is sublimated like a solid instantly becoming a gas. This is the sculpture of the Minimalists—geometric abstractions that maximize the viewer's evolving experience of space, translated back into the forms of everyday life. Essential objects for the domestic environment, if not its very essence.

Earlier I remarked on the effective hint at the presence of the maker's hand via some small, self-consciously placed details. A walnut dining set that dominates the center of the gallery employs these marks in an interesting way. The detail is a patch, or dutchman, that in the work-a-day world would be used to fill a natural imperfection or a mistake. McMakin's choice to include these perfectly crafted but apparently unnecessary marks as evidence of "craftsmanship" is at once beautiful and bewildering. His "explanation" for these patches is the sustainable use of materials, but they also refer to the prime directive of Modernism—truth to materials—and bring to mind a Modernist reverence for wood as expressed in the work of, say, George Nakashima. To me this is clearly a diversionary tactic, a linguistic distraction that suggests a subversive pun on Modernist craft values and ideology. Beneath the surface lies a more interesting historical allusion. In his hilarious *Knotty Pine Box* from 1966, H. C. Westermann carefully inlaid imperfections into a clear pine box, undermining assumptions of the preciousness of nature and the values of craftsmanship. It is nice to find a little humor in *A Slat-back Chair.* But these marks serve a deeper purpose in further blurring the boundaries between the realm of the designer and that of the workman. The resulting experience, particularly for one conversant in the history, materials, and techniques that are furniture's language, is circuitous and confounding but one that engages me on a delightful variety of unexpected levels. The dining set is perhaps the piece most alienated from its role in the gallery setting and this dialogue serves to effectively address that distance for the viewer/user.

The exhibition returns to more purely formal concerns with a series of individually presented objects loosely abstracted from the slat-backed chair form. These pieces attempt a more complex conceptual leap with mixed success. A "negative" chair grows from the wall, subverting the solidity of its partner sitting in "normal" space. Two chairs nested, mirrored, create a Siamese hybrid, *Nightstand.* These pieces differ from others in that they rely on linguistic and formal conceits. While clever in concept, each lacks the power to elicit a response via the viewer's imagining of the physical experience of use. In the first case the chair forms have been too dematerialized, and have become too abstract. In becoming the "idea of a chair" they lose their familiar iconic identity. "Conceptual" furniture often labors under its detachment from the physical imagination. We carry this imagining with us and bring it to the work, completing it, participating in its effectiveness and meaning. This is the potential that McMakin's most successful work possesses. *Nightstand,* however, is less successful due to its reliance on a purely visual idea of "chairness." It engages the viewer from a distance as a visual pun, ignoring the vital experiential depth of the haptic and tactile parallels to visual imagination. Pye's delicate balance of distance and empathy is lost.

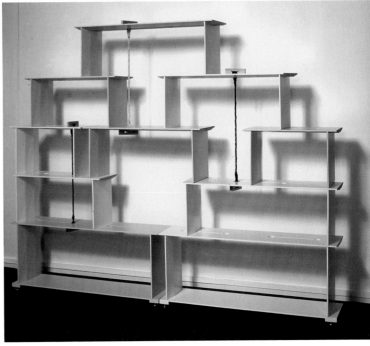

Nesting Bookcase (2001)
Joe Scanlan
Wood, fabric, paint, nylon (lavender and white)
142 x 99 x 18.5 cm (x2)
Courtesy Joe Scanlan and Galerie Micheline Szwajcer

A final piece succeeds, however, in this regard. A low excavation through the drywall and studs of the gallery wall ends in a small opening through which one sees the legs of chairs and of passing gallery visitors. My imagination attempts to recreate the opposing view, remembering a simple chair, a mirrored space between its back slats, in conversation with its partners. But the mirrored space I remember turns out to be the void I'm looking through. No punch line, not even a title (Untitled). I'm left with an image of a chair sitting against a wall. Mundane. Not even a memorable chair! But the image in my mind is irreconcilable in space and time. I feel my grounding slip. I'm nowhere and everywhere.

Roy McMakin has shown us a chair and stated, "This is not a chair." Not that long ago, another artist said the same thing about a pipe, challenging the notion that everyday objects belong to objective reality—that they mean what we see. *A Slat-back Chair* is that kind of experience. Who'd have guessed that furniture could do that?

REVIEW

Old Brown Furniture

John Townsend lights up the Metropolitan

by Michael Podmaniczky

Those who are not enthusiasts of antique furniture can be forgiven if they find an exhibition of 18th century furniture from Newport, RI, well, boring. Old brown furniture with little ornamentation or other decoration to jolt the eye and capture the imagination may not fare well when measured against contemporary furniture or even furniture of the same era but made in a more stylistically freewheeling regional center, Philadelphia for example. Newport furniture is an acquired taste

requiring some serious time spent in front of the objects and not a little reading time.

When someone refers to "Newport furniture," they usually are talking about a narrow parameter of time and style. Where "Boston furniture" is everything from Pilgrim era to 19th century revival, Newport is not distinctive for very early or very late furniture. It is pretty much limited to the last three-quarters of the 18th century, encompassing the Queen Anne, Chippendale, and Federal styles, roughly the late Baroque, Rococo, and early Classical periods in art historical terminology.

Further limiting the playing field is the way Newport cabinetmakers interpreted these styles. The signature of the Queen Anne period may be reduced to the idea of form in space. The aesthetic of curved, undulating profile, form, and volume had been formalized by William Hogarth's study of what he called the "line of beauty," an S-shaped cabriole or ogee curve. Throughout decorative art history, repetitive C and S curves were incorporated into furniture in standardized combinations. The Queen Anne style represents a zenith of this aesthetic. Chairs of this period are most recognizable for their cabriole front legs, rounded shoulders, serpentine seat rails, and solid vase or baluster-shaped back splats. Every perspective reveals a combination of S and/or C curves. Carving was minimal, often a fairly realistic scallop shell and perhaps a little leafage, but for the most part, it was the form, not the decoration that really drove the style in America (absent the costly and time consuming realistic bunches of flowers, fruits, and dead animals so popular as added ornament in Britain and the Continent). If a Queen Anne chair is back-lit so that only its outline and volume can be perceived, the power and impact of the design is hardly diminished.

Boston cabinetmakers applied this notion to case furniture by adding blocking to the fronts of chests of drawers and desks. The in-and-out shaping of these facades played off the undulating chairs, though more on a two-dimensional plane. The Boston kettle-shaped "bombe" (French, "swelled") desks and chests of drawers carried the form-in-space undulation to the entire piece. Newport cabinetmakers saw and raised Boston to an aesthetic height unmatched by the latter, or any

other regional center for that matter. In fact, the good people of Newport were so satisfied with their Baroque look, they never bothered to make the transition to what passed for the Rococo in America (contrasted with a much more wild and crazy, whimsical, even fantastical European expression).

Skipping the Rococo

While Philadelphia, New York, Boston, Charleston, and other points south simplified the overall undulation of the Queen Anne while decorating the Rococo surface with fussy, profile-blurring carved ornament, Newport pressed on with only subtle refinements of what they had already established. The City by Narragansett Bay skipped the Rococo, eventually rejoining the other centers in the transition to the Federal or early Classical style promoted by such designers as Sheraton, Adam, and Hepplewhite.

Further compacting the study of Newport furniture is the dominance of one cabinetmaking family, represented by the merging of two families, Goddard and Townsend. Intermarriage and family apprenticeships created an extended but nonetheless tightly woven web of connections

facing page: Bureau table—Newport outdid Boston with this design, adding the distinctive scallop shells and ogee, rather than straight, bracket feet. These undulating, six-footed chests display a heavily concentrated dose of extreme craftsmanship.

The Museum of Fine Arts, Houston. The Bayou Bend Collection, Gift of Miss Ima Hogg, B.69.91. Joseph McDonald Photography.

Editor's Note—*Mike Podmaniczky is senior furniture conservator at Winterthur and associate Winterthur professor at the University of Delaware, and also chair of the Furniture Studio Editorial Advisory Board. Mike represents a welcome new breed of scholar we had not known until quite recently. Having worked as a furniture maker, patternmaker, and boat builder, his historical scholarship is informed by his own technical mastery of the woodworking and furniture-making crafts—when Mike suggests how the old guys might have made something, he's very probably correct. And although he is understandably starry-eyed about the great works of the 18th century, which surround him every day at Winterthur, he is equally passionate about contemporary studio furniture, and extremely open and welcoming to contemporary makers who wish to learn more about our decorative arts heritage.*

The Metropolitan Museum has published a catalog of the exhibition, entitled John Townsend: Newport Cabinetmaker, *by Morrison H. Heckscher; look for ISBN 1-58839-145-0.*

—*John Kelsey*

among these craftsmen, whose multiple and overlapping relationships read like an American Kennel Club bloodline. As scholars have already done with other regional centers and their most notable craftsmen, Rhode Island furniture is currently being teased open by historians and curators, and the many less-well-known craftsmen are being given a modicum of recognition, but in the case of Newport, it is not unreasonable to assume attribution to some member of the Goddard/Townsend clan, or at least, someone who worked for them.

In the summer and fall of 2005, Morrison Heckscher, the Lawrence A. Fleischman Chairman of the American Wing at the Metropolitan Museum of Art, presented one fruit from this densely laden tree with the exhibition and catalogue titled *John Townsend: Newport Cabinetmaker.*

The Townsend exhibition and catalogue was a much welcomed addition to the sparse library of major publications on Newport furniture. Of the two books first off the tongue, Ralph Carpenter's *The Arts and Crafts of Newport Rhode Island 1640–1820,* and Michael Moses's *Master Craftsmen of Newport, The Townsends and Goddards,* only the latter is dedicated solely to furniture. Not only is Carpenter's book over a half-century old, but also it covers all the decorative arts, not just furniture. Moses is an economist and he approaches the subject like an engineer with a scalpel. He dissects the furniture to an extreme, but by doing so, he makes abundantly clear the talcum-fine distinctions that the connoisseur must sift in attributing a piece. The stuff all looks the same.

Block and Shell Reunion

Heckscher has done a great service in removing the "Where's Waldo" aspect of a broad-brushed Newport furniture exhibition by focusing on one of the big names in this Mormonesque familial group: John Townsend. John Townsend and John Goddard are arguably the two super-heavyweights of the family, and this exhibition permitted a relaxed opportunity to view a fully loaded installation of Townsend's work, from his earliest

flat-top high chest of drawers to an exquisite assembly of the finest Federal style straight-leg inlaid tables. But the real power in this exhibition lies with the extensive reunion of block and shell case furniture. It was a feast.

Although the exhibition would serve as an inspiration for any furniture maker, the catalogue is written more for the serious connoisseur and furniture scholar. There is little insight given to the nuts and bolts of Townsend's joinery beyond description, and in a few cases detailed photography. For example, Townsend's use of tongue-and-groove joined knee brackets on some of his straight-leg tables is noted. But the more nuanced description, of how one of the two mortise grooves was chopped long so that the bracket could be rotated into place after, rather than during table apron assembly, is not offered, nor is the delicate detail of wedging the extended mortise to lock everything in place after assembly. Another technical feature that could have used a more detailed examination is the Newport method of attaching tops to some of the low case pieces. The front edge of the top board is screwed from below to a cross-rail that joins the two sides, but the back edge is held down with two small butterflies of wood that are effectively double-ended dovetails (the dovetail version of a slip-tenon or floating tenon). Oriented vertically, these are fitted without glue into half-blind dovetail mortises in the back cross-rail, with mirrored mortises cut into the back edge of the top and retained by the back boards. In this way, case tops were allowed to float front

right: High chest of drawers—Conventional wisdom has it that the best carving was placed as close to eye level as a furniture form permitted. Rather than carving applied to the tympanum or "scroll board" as was the custom in Philadelphia and New York, Townsend followed Newport convention by continuing his drawer façade in shaped paneling, and relegated carving literally to knee level and down. Here is seen the interface of the two heaviest influences on Newport, a Boston inspired pediment, and claw feet that have been appropriated from New York City.

Private collection, a promised gift to the Metropolitan Museum of Art, New York. Bruce Schwarz, The Photograph Studio, The Metropolitan Museum of Art.

Knee carving and carved shells—For those who have only a casual interest in Newport furniture, these say it all. Only the connoisseur can or cares to distinguish between the slightly nuanced versions of neo-Greco knees and compulsively perfect scallop shells of Newport. Both examples anticipate the perfectionism of 19th century carving rather than reflect back on the liveliness and spontaneity of 18th century Rococo carving.

Eric Noah, New York, New York. Bruce Schwarz, The Photograph Studio, The Metropolitan Museum of Art.

to back so as to avoid splitting under extreme environmental changes.

Another technical point that actually rises above the level of construction detail is the curious nature of long-leg case construction. In the previous William and Mary stylistic period, cases were put together as dovetail-boxes-with-drawer-openings. Upper cases were oriented vertically (as they will continue to be in subsequent periods), but lower cases and en suite dressing tables were dovetailed in a horizontal orientation. The front was then worked out in various seat-of-the-pants ways to produce the requisite drawer openings, but apropos this discussion, legs were applied after the case construction was complete. Bulbous turned legs with integral round tenons were socketed into the

corners of the case that were first beefed up with interior glue blocks to provide ample wood for boring the round mortise.

With the advent of the Queen Anne style and the introduction of the carved and shaped cabriole leg, virtually every design center wrestled briefly with how to apply the new, unturned and thus square-posted leg to the old dovetailed box case construction. All centers quickly moved to the new construction method of lengthening the leg post to the top of the case and making it integral to the box construction by virtue of receiving the sides, backs and most of the front elements via mortise-and-tenon. That is, all except Newport, and John Townsend. Newport cabinetmakers continued to dovetail their cases together and fit their square-posted legs to the inside corners of the cases, held in place with glue blocks and wedges. Aesthetically, this riffed off of the stark, unfigured choice of woods, and the flat or undulating but unornamented surfaces by avoiding the busy-ness of opposing figure patterns and draw pegs (not to mention the inevitable splitting of wide side boards restrained by the cross-grain orientation of the leg posts) that became the norm everywhere else in America. These are sometimes misleadingly called "detachable" legs (just what you would want in a high chest of drawers!) despite the glue blocks and wedge, or the technique is attributed to a desire for compact shipping— certainly a benefit, but hardly the driving agent. Rather, this is yet another indication of virtually unshakable craft traditionalism.

These major as well as minor construction details, virtually unique to Newport, are noted, and occasionally pictured, but more in-depth discussion would have been welcomed by today's cabinetmaker. But why complain, when they have been left for a more technical essay yet to be written by someone who will owe the opportunity to Heckscher's excellent catalogue. (It should be noted that because of much weightier responsibilities at the Metropolitan Museum, Heckscher, and we, owe a debt of gratitude to his research assistant and co-author, Lori Zabar.)

China table—As with all his furniture, Townsend constructed this table with compulsive attention to perfection in every detail, but oddly juxtaposed organically flowing fretwork in the gallery with Chinese inspired open-work brackets and cross-stretchers that have been jokingly referred to as "Deco-rococo."

Winterthur Museum, Winterthur, Delaware, Museum Purchase, 58.37.
Bruce Schwarz, The Photograph Studio, The Metropolitan Museum of Art.

The catalogue photography is superb, offering breathtaking overall images of Townsend's furniture as well as many shots of details, undersides, and backs, a phenomenon unheard of before the influences of scholarly furniture makers and conservators were admitted to the Academy over the past 40 years. Heckscher is a strong advocate of integrating the technical and art historical, and he showed this interest with wit and charm. He displayed two case pieces upside down and with drawers withdrawn for close inspection, under an 18th century painting of Caribbean colonialist sea captains carousing in a tavern room accented by overturned chairs.

He was so taken by the bon mot that he included an image of the painting in the catalogue. He even went so far as to install a John Cederquist trompe l'oeil "Newport" high chest, though he placed it three steps away, just outside the gallery entrance (and not in the catalogue—there are some places the Metropolitan Museum just won't go). These exhibition details added immeasurable interest to what could be, to some of the public, a dreary installation of Old Brown Furniture. Heckscher has the experience and sensitivity to know how to draw everyone in, no matter the subject.

Very Little Art

But why should a collection of such incredibly masterful furniture be considered dreary? Repetition is one reason. Despite the feast offered by an entire wall of lined-up block-and-shell bureau tables, there is very little art involved. The materials are exceptional: dense, fine-grained Island mahogany. But by definition, and more importantly, maker's choice, this mahogany exhibits minimal figure (the wild and crazy stuff all went to Philadelphia). The execution of joinery and carving, to borrow a phrase from the catalogue, "has a machinelike precision." Indeed. I could imagine a group of, say, 19th century steam engine or firearm enthusiasts stumbling across this exhibition and finding themselves even more entranced than furniture scholars or contemporary studio furniture makers. This stylistically constipated furniture is not art, and Townsend was not an artist.

Machine-like Precision

Anyone who has ever carved (or more likely, attempted to carve) a Newport shell knows that nothing else from that period in American furniture is remotely related. Where a carver can hide in the looseness and relative frivolity of Philadelphia Rococo carving, the "machinelike precision" of Newport's intensely constrained shells and knee-carvings demands an entirely different mind- and skill-set.

Were Townsend alive and working today, I dare say he would be, at the very least, a tool-and-die maker. He would work for someone like Raytheon or NASA, making intricate rocket parts—or more likely, he would have moved up to Providence and settled in as the master technical support machinist for the engineering department's prototype shop

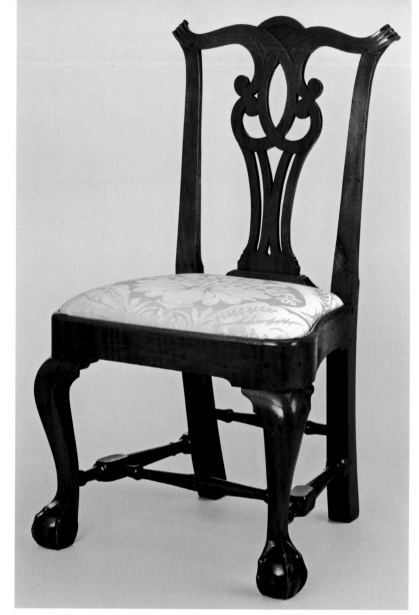

"Chippendale"-style side chair—The stolidness of this chair is overwhelming. It was built when the Baroque was giving way to some degree of Rococo frivolity—everywhere but Newport. The details of claw feet, pierced splat and "eared" crest all get their boxes checked as indicative of the new style, despite the overwhelmingly anti-Rococo spirit projected by heavy proportions, regimented decoration, throw-back stretchers and serpentine seat rail.

Newport Restoration Foundation, Newport, Rhode Island, 1999.537.1. Bruce Schwarz, The Photograph Studio, The Metropolitan Museum of Art.

at Brown University. He is about as far from the self-expressive furniture artist of today as he could possibly be. The scary part is that he wasn't unique. The rest of the family was virtually the same, they and all their furniture.

For those material culture scholars who study objects in order to tease out the nature of the society from whence they come, Heckscher has presented an alarmingly conservative, if not

"Federal"-style side chair—Townsend, and his contemporaries, were eventually forced into transition by the Classical style which could surely be interpreted in a more-or-less staid manner, but not saddled with characteristics of an earlier design period. Townsend's meticulous approach to carving was ideally suited to the new carved decoration, allowing him to flourish aesthetically at the end of his career.

Winterthur Museum, Winterthur, Delaware, Museum Purchase, 60.112.
Bruce Schwarz, The Photograph Studio, The Metropolitan Museum of Art.

after all. They weren't shoving this furniture down the throats of the locals (although the records of massive numbers of export pieces they made could indicate a weak home market). So what are we to understand of this place that less than 100 years later became a paradigmatic Gomorrah of Gilded Age excess and self-indulgence? Did the schizophrenic implications of a lifestyle and an economy based so fundamentally on slaves and booze cause the Yankee Protestants and Quakers of the community to retreat into a defensive, lockstep conservatism? It is fascinating to consider the irony of a town with this apparent personality heading toward The Breakers, Marble House, and the influence of New York City excess less than 75 years later. Neither the exhibition nor the catalogue goes anywhere near these sociological questions, but of course that was not the intent.

From simply an object-oriented perspective, this exhibition is important for bringing together such masterpieces of American furniture. The quality and choice of materials and the technical execution of the pieces is unsurpassed by any other region or city. But what of the art? If anything, Townsend becomes even more stolid and rigid over time. Chairs and tables become heavier and blockier, rather than more elegant and sophisticated, until they are finally, if only partially, rescued by the transition to the inherently more delicate Federal style. And the precise, Neo-Greco cabriole knee carving so uncharacteristic to what was being done during the Rococo period in other cities (remember, Newport skipped that part) did serve Townsend well as he made the transition to the Classical style where precision and exacting detail were so necessary for successful carving.

reactionary, time and place. A great deal of energy has been expended over the past few years ferreting out minutiae as to the origins and attributions of Newport furniture that now seem to be tied up more with New York or Boston. And the general stylistic influences of the two regions on such things as pediment shape or number of card table legs has been noted, but the more humanistic implications of Newport furniture have been lost. What on Earth was going on there? The Townsends and Goddards weren't tangoing with themselves,

detail of *Lion Bench*, p. 119

Judy Kensley McKie: Work That Stands As If It Always Was

2005 Furniture Society Award of Distinction

Introduction by Michael Hurwitz, photo captions by Judy McKie with Amy Forsyth

Judy McKie's work has always struck a universal chord within viewers, having an accessible presence that can feel both as familiar and as alarming as a déjà vu experience. Though it may sometimes remind us of the material culture of primitive societies, it more importantly stands as an icon of our collective unconscious. It stands there as if it always has.

Perhaps the reason we're so ready to receive her work is because it's already part of us. As viewers we experience a permeability that we don't feel with other work. This quality is fundamental

to its attractiveness. It's as if we're interacting with a magnetic field that leaves us no choice.

I first met Judy 27 years ago during my last year in school at Boston University. Right after graduation I joined the cooperative workshop where she was also a member, and over the next six years we not only became good friends, but also she became a tremendous inspiration to me. In a young field where a little ambition could take one a long way, it was inspirational to work with someone whose only ambition seemed to be to make honest work. Early on she stopped taking commissions, afraid not only of the impact it might have on her designs but also because she sincerely did not want to risk disappointing the client.

Judy has always had a sense of clarity about the essence of each project, and she always had a determination to get it right. This sometimes meant re-carving, refinishing, and re-refinishing before it ever left the studio, and it didn't leave unless it was right. And by right I mean that it was at peace with itself and all of its elements were consistent with, and supportive of, its essential nature.

She has always maintained a humble modesty. I remember around 1981 or '82, Judy was working with one part-time helper, trying to keep up with demand. She got a call from a major New York gallery promising more work and more money, and that with them she would get bigger and bigger. Her response was, "But I don't want to get bigger, I want to get smaller."

In spite of her desire to stay small, in the years since then Judy has produced a formidably huge body of work. She has had about a dozen solo exhibitions, participated in several dozen group shows, has won two National Endowment for the Arts fellowships and a Tiffany Foundation award, and her work is in many public and private collections including the museums of fine arts in Philadelphia, Houston, Albuquerque, Toledo, and Boston, plus the permanent collection at the White House. Recently, she helped establish and furnish the Garden of Peace in Boston—a major project commemorating the victims of violent crime.

Dragonfly Chest (1987)
Carved limewood;
60 in. high x 48 in. wide x 20 in. deep.
Photo: David Caras

Each dragonfly is the handle of a separate drawer. I've done a lot of pieces like this because I dislike it when the handles have nothing to do with the furniture they're on. You pick from a catalogue, from whatever is available, and it's horrible on the chest. You spend all this time and energy making something nice, only to have the handles ruin it. It seems to me that the handles should be figured out beforehand, as part of the design, and not as an afterthought. The handles can make it more beautiful. But if you don't think about the handles and the hardware until the end, you back yourself into a corner and don't have much to choose from.

Michael Hurwitz makes furniture in Philadelphia. Hurwitz' introduction is taken from his remarks introducing McKie during The Furniture Society's 2005 Award of Distinction program at its San Diego conference. Amy Forsyth, who teaches furniture design and making at Lehigh University in Bethlehem, PA, interviewed McKie for the captions during fall 2005.

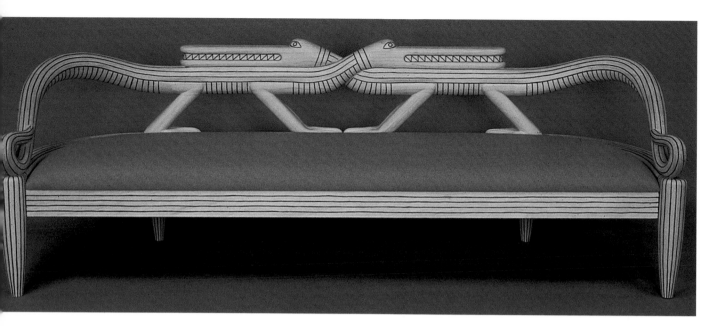

above: Lizard Couch (1987)
Mahogany, carved and bleached;
30.5 in. high x 90 in. wide
x 25 in. deep.

right: Dog Table #2 (1984)
Carved walnut, glass;
34 in. high x 60 in. wide x 18 in. deep.

In the lizard couch the animals interlock. I needed something big enough to lean back on. So by putting the heads on top of each other, there was enough surface area for that—if they had just met in the middle it would have been too low and uncomfortable. With the dog table, the bones make stretchers to hold up the tabletop. Putting two animals together gave me enough parts under the table to hold the glass. In the first version of this table, I had the head and the tail balancing the table top and the bone at the bottom of their feet. The tails came up, took a wide curve, and went flat to hold up the top. But there was too much flex in the tail—it wasn't strong enough—and there was a little bit of wobble in the glass too. So I redid it with the bone at the top and moved the legs apart, making the table more stable. These are all practical considerations, I'm a very practical person. When I design something I think about the form of the animal, consider which part could hold up the tabletop, that the wood will expand and contract. Many of the design constraints are wood issues that mean things have to be readjusted.

When I start designing something, I'm not thinking about furniture, because it's too confining. I just draw. Sometimes I'll draw floral imagery, though rarely landscapes because I prefer things that have a more graphic quality. I'm really attracted to animals, because I want to bring the furniture to life. So I'll start by just drawing animals. I don't want to be thinking about how to put something together or whether it will work or not. So then if I come up with an animal form that I like, I'll think about how it could be used in a piece of furniture, whether it could be an armrest or whether it could support something if I make the tail a little longer, or if I put two of them together. So that's the process, it comes from drawing rather than from furniture.

I was sitting in a living room somewhere, looking at a Chippendale fretwork mirror, how it was constructed, and I realized that you could do something fun with that. The burning mirror was a take-off on Chippendale fretwork. A gigantic miter is not stable and it'll start to crack and fall apart when the wood contracts and expands. But Chippendale fretwork had very small mitered corners and a lot of surface area for design, so there's a woodworking reason for making them that way. I like to work in very simple formats—that's why Parsons tables are great, there's a big surface to decorate. I work in two ways, either a flat, graphic surface decoration, or very three dimensional, like the dog table.

I did the original *Helping Hands Bowl* out of wood, and gave it to my husband, Todd, for his birthday. I thought it would be nice cast, so I borrowed the bowl back and the foundry did a casting from it. I designed the bowl by holding my own hands in different positions and trying to make things out of them. I think abstracted hands can be very beautiful, and because hands do useful things, there are all kinds of possibilities. The little bowl is like an offering. It's nice to think of all the different ways hands help you do things, and so a series would be fun—I have hands designed as bookends. I don't know if I'll build them or not, but the ideas are endless. After that, maybe I'll have to do something using feet.

top:
Burning CF Mirror (2004)
Carved basswood
with gold leaf;
35 in. high x 22 in. wide
x 1 in. deep.
Photo: Dean Powell

left:
Helping Hands Bowl (2001)
Cast bronze;
2 in. high x 7.25 in. wide
x 4.75 in. deep.
Photo: Dean Powell

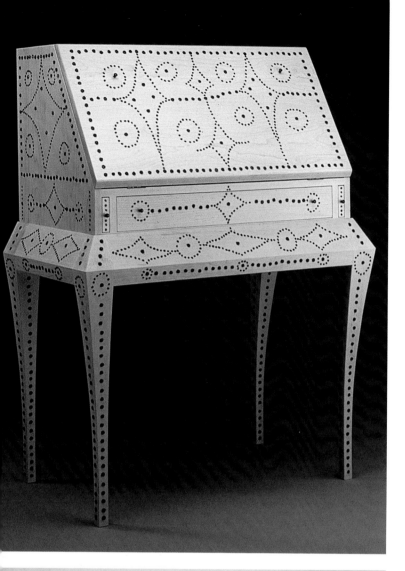

left: *Lady's Writing Desk* (2004)
Maple, nails; 44 in. high x 30 in. wide x 20 in. deep.
Photo: Dean Powell

below: Aquarium Chest (1997)
Basswood, paint, metal;
36 in. High x 35.5 in. wide x 24 in. deep.
Photo: Greg Heins

For the desk, I wanted to make an object that would be very ladylike, refined and delicate and elegant, and then to slam nails into it. I wanted the nails to be a little bit startling. It should look at first like a pretty little pattern, but then when you get up close, it's made out of iron nails, which are not delicate at all. And the pattern I drew was not regular and perfect. I drew it very carefully on the piece and put each nail in very carefully, but the idea was to have it look as if I had just sort of whacked them in there. I couldn't actually do it that way, because if just one nail had ended up in the wrong place, it would have been thousands of dollars and months of work down the drain. I had hired somebody to build the desk, so it's already expensive, and that doesn't include the ideas and the drawings and figuring it all out. The nails continue on into the inside. They're in the cubbyholes and the drawers.

The *Aquarium Chest* was made at a different time, but also used nails. When I first started decorating my furniture, I made a list of every possible way I could think of to alter a piece of wood, by carving it, or using nails as a pattern, or whatever. And I have given this exercise to students on the rare occasions when I have taught. I figured I would try to do every one of the things on my list before I die. I've gotten to most of them.

This was the last piece I made for a show and I felt like I worked on it fast—I didn't have the time to make sure everything was coming out just right. It's rare when I feel as if I don't have control over the piece. But the idea was to make a chest on a base that was part of a found glass-top table. I knew I wanted to use the nails and have the frame tie it all together. I was unable to be as careful with it as I am with almost everything else I've ever made—I know when it leaves that everything is in the right place. With this one I felt that some of the nails were not in the right place but I had to send it out anyway. But I saw it again recently in the collection of the person who bought it, and it looks much better than I had thought—it looked fine.

The *Ribbon Cabinet* is one in a series of six cabinets in the same format. I like the idea of making a pattern or a design that doesn't repeat itself exactly. It's a repeat pattern, but it's thrown off so it's not so easily recognized—it's the idea of something not being seen all at once nor immediately understood. The design almost repeats, but not quite. That's what's so beautiful about African patterns, that they're unpredictable. That's what makes them interesting. A lot of European patterns are so perfect that you take one look and you've seen the whole thing. Often I'll just mess around during one of my drawing sessions, I'll just make patterns and find places to use them later. Like the table, for instance. I did the design for something else and then I did a number of variations on a theme. One of the cabinets is a variation on the design of the table. My proportions are determined by eye, not by a system. I feel like somehow if you do it by eye you know if it's right. The cabinets are very elongated because I wanted to make something long and narrow. I always thought of them as bathroom cabinets, but big ones, because I had a place for one in my house. Now my house is full of furniture, but until recently, everything I've always imagined making had a place in my own house. Not that I would keep it, but I had to know that I would want to live with it forever before I would bother to build it.

right: Ribbon Cabinet (2000)
Carved mahogany;
50.5 in. high x 19.5 in. wide x 5.25 in. deep.
Photo: Dean Powell

Table with Pattern (1995)
Carved walnut, oil
and pigment;
30 in. high x 96 in. wide
x 35.5 in. deep.
Photo: Charles Mayer

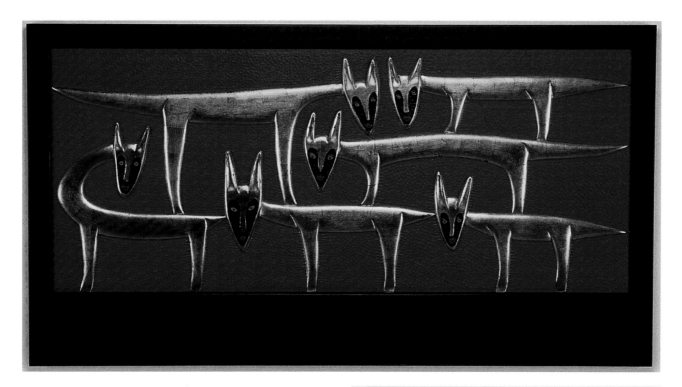

above: Watching Dogs Headboard (1991)
Maple, carved with gold leaf and paint;
32 in. high x 60 in. wide x 1.5 in. deep.

right: Mirror with Birds (1991)
Carved limewood;
30 in. high x 28 in. wide x 1.5 in. deep.
Photo: David Caras

I made a whole series of small mirrors in big frames
as a chance to focus on graphics, to make images on
the surface and have fun, instead of building a whole
piece of furniture that needs decorations on every
side. I did six or eight of these mirrors and they all
had different images on them. I had just been to Italy,
looking at 13th century religious paintings. The
gold leaf on those paintings was amazing, used in
combination with intense blue—they were so beautiful
together that I needed to use that combination of colors
in a piece of furniture. I don't know where the blackbirds
came from, but I started in my usual way, establishing
a format and doing a million drawings. I have a stack
of possibilities that I've never used in my file. I made
all the mirror frames at once and then used some
of the designs. My woodworking and my objects
are really simple, there's nothing complicated,
they're as simple as I can get them to be. Over time
I've learned how to do them right, it's not as if they're
going to fall apart or anything, but it doesn't interest
me to build really complicated pieces of furniture that
are mostly about woodworking—my work is more
about the imagery. And the imagery is what makes
it complicated and takes the most time.

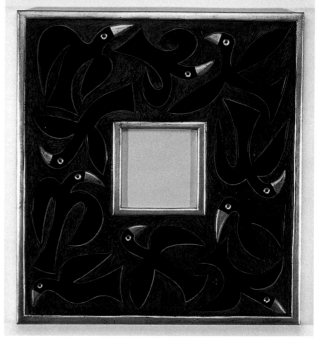

That headboard format was similar to the mirrors—
a chance to do a relief carving, something that's almost
just a painting in a frame. I didn't have to worry much
about constructing a piece of furniture, you just shove
your bed in front of it. It was really just another format
where I could do anything I wanted inside the frame.
I did a totally plain one, with those dogs, just in wood,
and then I did this one as a total contrast to it, then
a few more variations, just like the mirrors.

above: Monkey Chair (1994)
Cast bronze on walnut base;
36 in. high x 25 in. wide x 25 in. deep.
Photo: Scott McCue

below: Lion Bench (1994)
Cast bronze; 17 in. high x 72 in. wide x 17 in. deep.
Photo: Scott McCue

Casting bronze gave me the opportunity to work three-dimensionally in ways that would be difficult to do in wood, and also to make things for outdoors, which you really can't do out of wood. I use a material called signboard to make the model for the castings. I've used plaster or wood, but signboard is very light and doesn't dull your tools. I love animal imagery, and there's only so much you can do under a table, so it's really fun to think about what kinds of animals could be used in a chair.

In the *Lion Bench* I wanted to create something that happened within a rectangle so it would be very straightforward and benchlike, but was also a complete animal. I never use part of an animal, like a claw foot—that just doesn't work for me. The challenge of the *Lion Bench* was to have it be both a rectangle and a lion. It shouldn't feel like the lion is completely in the wrong shape. The legs had to be the right distance apart, the tail where it's supposed to be—like burrowing into the form to release the lion. On the other hand, the lion wants to be wrapped around the form, with surface tension. The challenge is always to make a complete piece of furniture that is also a complete animal. The *Monkey Chair* is one of the few pieces where there's a base and the animal forms rest on top of it. Occasionally that happens, but I like to have the whole thing function as the complete figure.

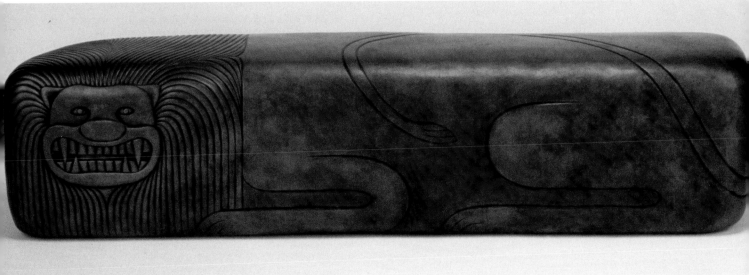

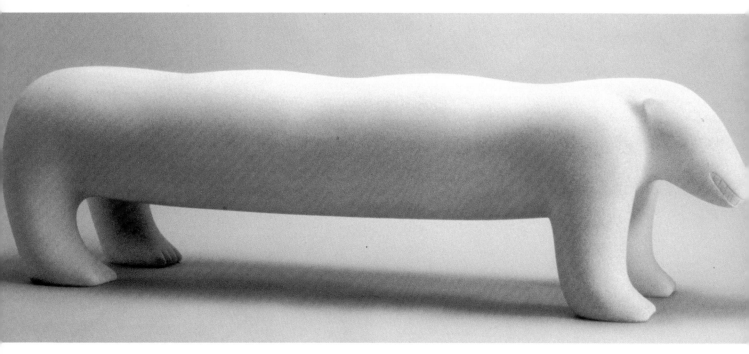

Polar Bear Bench (1997)
Carved marble;
20 in. high x 72 in. Wide x 20 in. deep.
Photo: Greg Heins

When I designed the polar bear, I needed to come up with the appropriate material—cold-feeling, from the Arctic, snowy, like winter time. Marble has a crystalline sparkle that feels like snow. There are two of these—one in Florida, and one in an apartment in New York, not very snowy places.

I do think about abstracting things, I don't want them to be realistic. Once something is described too completely, you've been given so much information that it almost doesn't interest you anymore. But when something isn't quite all there and you leave enough blank spaces or exaggerations, the viewer has to fill it in. I don't think the grizzly bear is as successful as the polar bear, because there's too much information, it got too realistic. He's goofy and ingratiating, a very friendly grizzly bear, almost too cute, like a teddy bear, except that his mouth is so close to his nose and the teeth are sharp. I got the stance, the legs are a little ding-toed, there's that hump behind the back, I tried to make it as much of a grizzly bear as possible, which is not what I usually try to do—I usually try to keep it from being so specific. I prefer the *Cat Bench,* which is maybe a cat and maybe something you've never seen before. To me, that is more interesting. Unlike the grizzly, which has fur, with the cat I used abstract patterns not relating to any animal at all—tribal marks that aren't fur, but represent it, a leaf-like pattern that would make the ear more interesting to look at; less specifically a cat's ear.

The eyes are eye-like without specifically representing cat's eyes. The clients wanted a cat, but allowed me to abstract it. I worked out all the forms in a drawing.

The *Cat Bench* was done for a public library in Cambridge. They wanted three different benches, but I knew that within the budget I could only afford to make one. The pragmatic solution was to design it so you could swivel the head and tail around. That way I could get them looking at each other and interacting, but we only had to make one mold, which is always the biggest expense.

I'm very pragmatic—that's why I always make furniture, never fine art objects. I'm not tempted to do something non-functional. But now as I run out of new things to try, new kinds of furniture to make, I start thinking maybe I'll just make an elephant or something. But ultimately that doesn't interest me. The real challenge is to try to make something that is equally considered, all the aesthetic judgments have to work as if it were just a sculptural piece, and all the functional parts have to work as if it were just a piece of furniture. I cannot make an uncomfortable chair—it doesn't work for me. Even though the chairs I make might not look comfortable, they are all comfortable to sit in.

top: Grizzly Bear Bench (2002)
Cast bronze;
20 in. high x 72 in. wide x 20 in. deep.
Photo: Scott McCue

bottom: Cat Bench (2002)
Cast bronze;
33.5 in. high x 62 in. wide x 17 in. deep.
Photo: Scott McCue

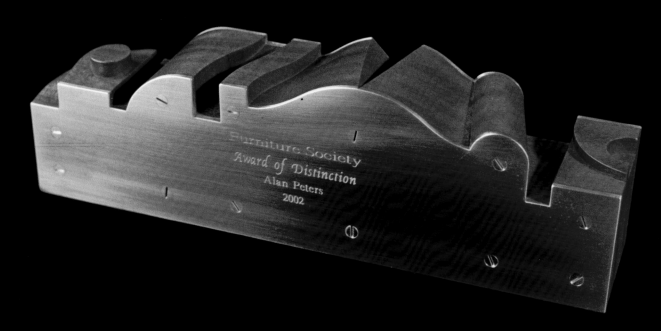

What is the Award of Distinction? How Can You Win One?

by Bebe Pritam Johnson

The idea for the Furniture Society's Award of Distinction program came about easily enough: if we wait for other institutions to honor the individuals who have been instrumental in shaping the field of studio furniture as we know it, then we could wait a long time. Far better, we thought, for The Furniture Society to put studio furniture and its superstars on center stage, and train our own spotlight on them. Armed with this mission and sense of organizational purpose, Ned Cooke and I proposed in 2000 that the society create an award of distinction program to honor individuals and institutions for lifetime achievement and overall contribution to the field. We said that anyone within the studio furniture community, except awards committee members, would be eligible for consideration providing they satisfied a few requirements. The society's board of trustees unanimously approved the recommendation at its June 2000 meeting in Toronto.

Requirements

While the awards program is blessedly free from a lot of rules, there are a few requirements for eligibility. The terms "lifetime" achievement and "overall" contribution are important. The award is not exclusive to makers, because the studio furniture community is composed of writers, museum directors, editors, curators, educators, collectors, dealers, publishers, and schools. At the same time, the board expressed a preference that each year's recipients include a maker, if a non-maker were to receive the award at the same time.

We also said that the recipient should attend the awards ceremony that takes place during the three-day annual conference; thus, there are no posthumous awards. We thought Furniture Society members would enjoy the chance to rub shoulders with these luminaries. Another rewarding aspect of the awards ceremony is that it takes place at a members' lunch on a conference Friday—everyone sitting and eating in one place, and on the same

plane, so to speak. Except for the first year, all of the award recipients have attended conferences, made artist presentations, and generally made themselves available to the membership. The exceptions occurred in 2001, when Peter Frid accepted the award on behalf of his ailing father, Tage Frid, and David Welter accepted on behalf of James Krenov, who chose not to attend, a decision he later said he regretted.

The Award Itself

In 2001, the awards committee put out a call for entries to members to come up with a design for our own "Oscar" or "Emmy," which very briefly was called the "Furnie." We selected Gord Peteran's design, which recalls the wood-and-metal hand planes of the 19th century. Peteran, who lives in Toronto, was commissioned to make an edition of ten award sculptures; in 2004, he was asked to make ten more. This time he came up with

a design, also to be fabricated in wood and metal, that resembles an old-fashioned folding rule.

The plan for the awards program is straightforward enough. A master of ceremonies introduces the presenter of the award. The presenter's task is to provide a 10-minute glimpse into the recipient's life and the nature of his or her contribution to studio furniture, without resorting to a resume recitation. We ask the presenter to tell us about the recipient in real terms and in personal ways. The recipient gives a five-minute acceptance talk, while someone else hefts the eight-pound wood-and-metal sculpture by Gord Peteran they have just been handed.

Bebe Pritam Johnson is one of two founding partners of Pritam and Eames gallery in East Hampton, New York, which specializes in showing and marketing studio furniture. She is also a member of The Furniture Society advisory board and was instrumental in creating the Award of Distinction program.

facing page: Sculptor and furniture maker Gord Peteran of Toronto designed and made the award itself. This one, presented in 2002 to the British furniture maker Alan Peters, is from Peteran's first edition of ten award sculptures, which were inspired by a traditional moulding plane. In 2005 Peteran created a second version, shown being given to Judy McKie in the photo above.

above: 2005 award winner Judy McKie and presenter Michael Hurwitz, clearly pleased, show off the Peteran sculpture she was awarded during The Furniture Society's San Diego conference. Peteran derived the current series of awards from an old-style folding rule.

Awards Committee

At this point, the reader may wonder about the awards committee and who appointed them. As with all Furniture Society standing committees, the president of the board appoints the committee chair, and the chair gathers the committee members. Initially, it was a bit like the little brown hen in the farmyard that wants to bake a loaf of bread. The other barnyard creatures think it's a good idea, but they're too busy to help. Therefore, if you have the idea, and others agree on its value, you go about the business of developing it, financing it, and publicizing it. Make it happen. Ned Cooke of Yale University, Rosanne Somerson of Rhode Island School of Design, and Bebe Johnson made up the first awards committee. Today's committee—Ned Cooke, Rosanne Somerson, maker Michael Fortune, curator Michael Monroe, Bebe Johnson, and most recently, *Woodwork* magazine editor John Lavine—has more than 150 years of studio furniture experience under its collective belt and as such, it is a healthy reflection of the membership's diversity. The committee deliberates mostly by e-mail because it is a far-flung group working in different time zones. The discussions are understandably confidential. Beyond lifetime achievement and overall contribution, factors of balance enter into consideration, along with geography, gender, maker versus non-maker, and style of work. It is the task of the awards committee to recommend to the board the next year's award recipient(s) and presenter(s). To date, the board has supported the committee's recommendations.

As for award nominations, the names can come from the membership at large or, as has been commonly the case, from the committee members. Thus far, the candidates have been prominent,

Furniture maker Wendell Castle of Scottsville, NY, shares a moment with fellow award recipients Arthur (Espenet) Carpenter of Bolinas, CA, *(center)* and Sam Maloof of Alta Loma, CA, *(right)*, during lunch at the 2002 Tempe, AZ, conference. Tage Frid of Providence, RI, and James Krenov of Ft. Bragg, CA, also were honored that year; neither was able to attend the ceremony. Bebe Johnson and Ned Cooke, both instrumental in creating the awards program, chat in the background.

visible figures in the studio furniture world. There is nothing, however, that precludes consideration of a candidate with quiet credentials. For example, is there a high school shop teacher out there that we need to know about who has instilled the skills, the respect for material, and the enjoyment of the furniture making process to generations of secondary school students?

Awards 2001: Tempe, AZ

While it might have been better to have fewer awards the first year, something splendid occurred in the 95-degree Arizona heat in June 2001 when Grif Okie presented the award to his friend, Art Carpenter; Jonathan Fairbanks presented the award to his friend, Sam Maloof; Garry Bennett presented the award to his friend and colleague, Wendell Castle; Rosanne Somerson presented the

Index